UNDIAGNOSED

Charlie
Thank you

[signature]

Larry Brady

UNDIAGNOSED

losing the son I didn't know

TATE PUBLISHING & *Enterprises*

Published by Tate Publishing & Enterprises, LLC
127 E. Trade Center Terrace | Mustang, Oklahoma 73064 USA
1.888.361.9473 | www.tatepublishing.com

Tate Publishing is committed to excellence in the publishing industry. The company reflects the philosophy established by the founders, based on Psalm 68:11,
"The Lord gave the word and great was the company of those who published it."

Book design copyright © 2011 by Tate Publishing, LLC. All rights reserved.
Cover design by Amber Gulilat
Interior design by Joel Uber

Published in the United States of America
ISBN: 978-1-61739-446-1
1. Biography & Autobiography; Personal Memoirs
2. Self-Help; Substance Abuse & Addictions, General
11.01.04

DEDICATION

This book is dedicated to all mothers who so desperately sacrifice for their children. To my wife, Betsy, the mother of our five children, who worked so hard to understand why she could not save Chris. She never gave up in her efforts to change the outcome.

Also in recognition to Chris's brothers: David, Jim, Mike, and Ricky.

ACKNOWLEDGMENTS

There are so many people I would like to thank and acknowledge that have made an impact upon my life and the life of my family. From these individuals, Betsy and I received much encouragement during difficult times.

Jack Cates, minister and brother-in-law, who continued to give spiritual advice during very difficult times. Chris said his uncle Jack was one of the best men he ever knew; I thank him also for doing such a good job performing Chris's funeral.

To Clyde Ray, minister, friend, and brother-in-law, for always encouraging me, as well as speaking at Chris's funeral.

To Clarence Denny, minister and friend, for speaking at Chris's funeral.

To the late Byron Benson, minister, for being such a good friend, brother in Christ, and confidant, who always listened; I thank him also for singing at Chris's funeral.

To the Pintlala community for being such good neighbors and one of the greatest communities to raise children.

To my good friends and fellow Christians, Larry and Sara Bills, for helping make corrections in the book.

To Chama and Darphilla Sanez of Sanson, Panama, who lost two children and now have so much in common with us.

To Knox and Pat Norman, who also lost a son to suicide a year before us; this has brought the bond between us closer.

To our wonderful church family; for without this connection, life would have been more difficult.

To Bill and Norma Watts, who helped us, loved us, and were always there, thank you for your many years of friendship.

To my late parents, Lewis and Thelma Brady, who were simple people who lived simple lives. A number of Mom's poems are recorded in this book.

To my sisters: Dianne Craig, Sandra Boddie, Sharon Cates, Betty Simmons, Verba Lee Ray, Pat McCain, June Brown, and Daisy Anne Brady, who always encourage me, often asking when the book will be ready.

To my brother, Allen, who wrote the foreword, for encouraging me when I got bogged down.

To my late brother, James (Buddy) Lewis, who kept the Brady homeplace looking so beautiful.

To my sons: David, Jim, Mike, and Ricky, and their wives, Jenny, Yvette, Kim, and Melissa, who called me, offering support, and also took over for Mom and Dad during the death of Chris.

To our ten grandchildren, who are the bright spots in our lives.

To Tate Publishing, for taking a chance on this book and encouraging me every step of the way.

To the families who, on a daily basis, must deal with the same problems we dealt with. Be strong in the Lord and the power of his might.

Above all, I owe everything to my wife, Betsy, who suffered more during the last fourteen years of Chris's life. She never gave up on him. She has been my friend, lover, and companion for thirty-eight years. She is a true example of motherhood.

Most importantly, I thank my God and my Savior Jesus Christ for saving me and giving Betsy and me strength to travel through some very difficult years. With God, all things are possible.

TABLE OF CONTENTS

FOREWORD

"Why did you do it, Chris?"

This question marks the beginning of our family's struggle to understand the behavior of my nephew, Chris. It was a question that was repeated often as time went on. Questions, by their nature, require answers, but the answer to our question proved elusive. In our seemingly futile search for understanding, anger mounted as our level of frustration increased.

How can we deal with the bad things that someone does when we are at a total loss to understand why a person not only does bad things but persists in doing them?

When a person repeatedly violates the standards of conduct, it shows a lack of concern for the effects of his behavior on others. This apparent lack of regard offends everyone's sensibilities. Why can't a person show consideration for others by just doing the right thing? Why can't a person conduct himself in a normal manner? Is that too much to ask? How can a person not understand the devastating effects his behavior can have on those he claims to love? Our response might be, "A person wouldn't really do that—not if he loved them!"

It happens more frequently than we might realize. It is difficult to grasp the notion that a person may love others dearly but be incapable of preventing himself from hurting them repeatedly. Only when we accept the fact that it can happen and identify the causes of these behavioral disruptions does the answer to the frequently asked question "Why did you do it?" come to us.

What is normal behavior? Normal behavior is that which holds true to existing, accepted standards. Much of our code of conduct is passed to us by custom and tradition, sometimes altering over time. Our religious background and instruction reinforce, or even instill within us, a sense of what is right and wrong. Family and community standards shape us. Some might argue that our genetic code carries within it a certain sensibility of right or wrong. All of these factors come together into a societal system in which each of us has a clear understanding of right and wrong, good and bad.

When a person adheres to the system, he is called good. When a person refuses to adhere to the system, he is called bad. However, this may not always be accurate. Perhaps a person does bad things because of factors we are unaware of, not because he is willfully defiant to behavioral norms. Perhaps a person does bad things for reasons even he does not understand and is incapable of fully controlling on his own. Perhaps behavior is, in part, dictated by aberrations from physiological norms and not as a conscious decision to act out.

Some might say this is a cop-out and an ultra-liberal attempt to excuse a person's behavior. No! I don't think excuses help anyone, but answers and solutions do. Frequently, we see the effect of our behavior while never grasping the cause. It is the identification of cause and effect that helps provide solutions.

Substance and alcohol abuse can result in altered behavior, and we readily identify cause and effect with the solutions being obvious. Our understanding of dementia is increasing and leads to better treatments and, possibly someday, a cure. Many physiological disorders have symptoms that help identify the problem and are accepted as markers of a particular condition. Even the average or untrained person can recognize certain common ailments and their symptoms. However, we average people may sometimes fail to recognize symptoms as such, and these conditional indicators escape us. We may misunderstand behavioral problems as not being symptomatic of a physiological or mental disorder. This misunderstanding then leaves us confused and generates the "Why?" questions. "Why did you do it, Chris?" "What were you thinking, Chris?" "What am I going to do with you, Chris?"

The answers to these "Why?" questions were more fully realized in the months and years following Chris's death.

During his teen and young adult years, Chris's life had become a battlefield and involved us all. As family members, we could not escape it. This battle eventually ended in an abrupt and shocking fashion that left all us in stunned disbelief. As the smoke and confusion of that battlefield faded, from chaos, clarity began to emerge. Understanding developed, and the answers came.

We were confronted with the realization that the field of battle was broader than just that part in which we had been engaged. We could not see the greater part of the battle, for it had raged in Chris's mind.

For Chris, this was a battle of wanting to abide by society's standards—to be called "good" and to demonstrate his love for others. A battle he was losing because of abnormalities that affected his thinking and behavior—behavior that caused him to be classified as "bad" by the same standards that he too accepted as being normal and desirable.

Chris knew that he was on a collision course. A course, which, though he did not want to follow, he seemed incapable of altering. Like being pushed along the wrong lane going through Atlanta, boxed in by traffic and unable to affect a lane change, Chris found himself repeatedly doing things that he did not want to do. With this lack of control, the circumstances around him became increasingly difficult. Chris was prevented from doing the positive things that he wanted to do by his mental dysfunction and, further, by the difficulties created by it.

This battle in Chris's mind raged as the level of desperation and hopelessness increased until one fateful evening when Chris was driven to end it all. Driven to a place where be did not want to be and kept from doing the things he wanted to do—things that were good. Chris's final act was to jump from a staircase and end his life. Desperation had become a cord about his neck, and hopelessness the void beneath his feet. That final act may also be considered bad by our societal standards. The effect of it heaped even more grief on those whom he loved and did not want to hurt. Being "bad" does not explain Chris's final act, nor does it explain many of the other actions of his life.

This is a story of a family's attempt to find the explanations. Perhaps in its reading, some answers may present themselves to someone else who is asking a loved one, "Why did you do it?"

—Allen Anderson Brady

INTRODUCTION

Mama, I am sorry for what has happened, but I cannot handle life anymore. Please fight to see my kids. I love you, and always remember me. Love, Chris

A person never forgets a loved one's last words. They linger and are repeated over and over. When the last words are from someone who has taken their life, there are more questions than answers. We search our hearts and minds, questioning where we failed. What more could we have done? Why did we not recognize the symptoms? Were there things we should have seen? A voice cried out, and we failed to hear it.

On September 18, 2005, sometime in the midafternoon, our son, Chris, wrote these words. These words are forever embedded in our minds. An entire life summed up in twenty-nine words. Sitting there, we stared at the torn piece of paper the note was written on. I wondered what was going on in Chris's mind on this fateful afternoon. Looking back, I knew he was lonely. He was looking for someone to fill a void. He was agonizing over his children, for he had not seen them in a while. His telephone calls went unheeded. His world had closed in around him as though there was nowhere else to go. There was no one he could turn to, not even his mother. What thoughts filled his mind as he prepared to end it all? Who in their right mind writes, "Life is not worth living"? Life for people who live with mental illness becomes so complicated that they cannot find the answers they are looking for. They then turn to the only place they can find peace: death.

Betsy and I must have read those words a hundred times after the sheriff returned his letter to us. Over the next several weeks, we would read the letter over and over again to try to make some sense of why Chris took his life. It was as though the answer was within the letter itself. Perhaps it was because this was his handwriting, and we just wanted to be close to him. There seemed to be no answers, so we began searching for them.

The death of one's child is the single most devastating event that can happen to parents. There are no words in the human vocabulary to describe how one feels. It does not matter what their age is; it is extraordinarily devastating. Words escape me to express how I felt and what it has done to his mother. People always think, These things happen to other people.

We all experience, one time or another, some form of tragedy. Friends or family or church family all have been touched by death. But when it comes to the death of a child, this is a different matter.

Many times, I have picked up the newspaper in the morning and read of some tragedy that had come to some family—some event that has totally changed the course of their lives. Being a minister, it has been my responsibility to go to families and tell them their loved one would not be coming home. We turn the television on and hear of a tragedy that has befallen a family; a child in an accident; a son or daughter killed in action in a war in some faraway land. The realities set in that this can happen to me. It happens in faraway lands to other people other cultures, but when it does hit home, devastation is the word. That's putting it mildly. One all of a sudden feels sick. The body is filled with nausea and there is no controlling what happens next. The emotion spills out in the form of tears. One feels numb to everything around them, even to people who are there to help. One hears voices, but the words have no meaning.

We then began the blame game and started beating ourselves up, saying, "Where did we fail? Why did we not do more?" Why is this happening to us?" The questions were there; we just had no answers.

We did everything we could to be good parents, such as going to church every Sunday and teaching by example. I made statements like, "If my children smoke, it is not because they saw Betsy and me smoke. If they drink or curse or mistreat their mates, it is not because they saw us do it." Yes, we thought we were doing everything right.

This goes beyond the borders of money, prestige, power, and religion, because if money could have saved him, we spent it. We borrowed it, we sold things, and we maxed out our credit cards. Anything we could do to come to his rescue. We bailed him out of jail simply because we felt so guilty, thinking we were rescuing him. In the long run, it was the worst thing we could have done. We were filled with guilt because we thought we had let him down. Our son sitting in a jail cell was beyond our thinking, for we had the ability to get him out. He would beg us, saying, "Please get me out," during the phone call he was allowed.

The night of Chris's death, we cried a million tears and begged for answers. How does a family prepare for such a storm that comes so suddenly?

When the storm hit Sunday, September 18, 2005, zeroing in on the Brady house, it totally devastated our family. The news spread fast as others felt our loss. Neighbors began to pour through the gates of the Brady family homeplace to offer comfort.

Oh yes, we talked about this very day but hoped we would not have to deal with it. At what time in his life did Chris start having problems with mental illness, drugs, and anger, the things that brought him and our family so much suffering? When did it start?

In my ministry, I have taught Bible classes, preached sermons, and conducted funerals and weddings using the Bible to tell people how God is faithful and loving and kind and how he feels for the brokenhearted. A verse I always use is 1 Peter 5:7 (Kjv): "Casting all your care upon him; for he cares for you." God does care! God is a God of the mountains, as well as the valleys. We know he is! I do believe it with all of my heart, but there came times in my life when I would cry out, "Oh God, Why me? Why us?" In my solitude following the death of Chris, standing in some lonely, secluded spot, I wept thinking about what could've been. Standing at his grave several days after his death, looking at the fresh dirt and the flowers that had begun to dry up, I had a talk with him. I told him how sorry I was for not having done more.

"Chris, you remember when you told me, 'Daddy, you just don't understand'? Son, I am here telling you that I did not understand. There is so much your mother and I did not know." Betsy and I so desperately searched for a reason why all of this was happening to us and to our family. The tragedy is I wanted to help. I really wanted to help, but I couldn't help what I didn't understand.

We tried to understand more about the problems he was having so we would not become so angry when we couldn't deal with them anymore. Standing there, I talked to Chris as though he could hear me, and maybe he did. Maybe he saw my tears and my agony. I felt so useless and undone, and the guilt began to pour into my life. On the evening before the funeral, I wrote an article to be read by my brother-in-law, Jack Cates, which in part said, "I know life must move on, and somehow, some way, we must try to make some sense out of all of this."

Now it was me standing by my son's grave, crying, "Why? Why?"

The day came when my family was the focus of the conversation of the community. We were the ones on everyone's prayer list in the churches. We were the ones in the news, with people opening the paper and looking in the obituaries, only to see the name and the information about our son's death. It was the Brady's who now were the center of all the attention, when before, we were part of the ones giving the attention. We were not the ones comforting, but we were the comforted. It was our family who was devastated and had to make funeral arrangements.

This is the story of a family who agonized about things for which they had no answers. It's about a child who turned into a handsome young man who had so much promise but never reached the potential of what he could've been. His searching took him to places he never expected to go. Chris would endure a disease that would follow him into adult life—a disease that few of us understood, that affects more families than we want to admit. Parents are embarrassed to admit their son or daughter is a crack head or has mental illness.

Many books and periodicals have been written on how to cope with mental illness, and yet, it is difficult for families to find the right answer—an answer to a disease that steals dignity and destroys personality.

Then we had to deal with drugs that controlled every thought. They consume a person, often leaving the individual and the entire family in the gutter.

This is the story of a young man who had everything going for him, and yet, he felt life was not worth living. He was handsome, charming, and intelligent.

This is a story of a life cut short with a disease we did not understand. It was a disease one couldn't see, and there were no operations to cut out the infected area. No one could recognize it outwardly, for it does not leave a person with a deformed appearance. They are destroyed from the inside out. When treated, an individual can live a normal life and become a productive citizen. This is a disease that destroys relationships, leaving the individual exhausted and knowing not where to turn, and thus, the end results can be devastating.

When there are drugs on top of the mental illness one must deal with, life becomes very complicated. It is hard enough to deal with one without the other. As parents, we had to deal with both. Betsy and I have often said since Chris's death, "If we had only known he was not just another bad child, a bully, of sorts." It never crossed our minds there was something like this in our family.

Perhaps there's a family member of someone known to you, the reader, or even within your own family who's having some of these same struggles. People search for answers as to why their son or daughter acts the way he or she does. A child who becomes angry easily or pitches temper tantrums all the time might be a signal something is wrong. A big mistake parents make is being careful not to intrude on their son or daughter's privacy. If there was ever a big mistake made with Chris, it was here. If something is going on in the home, and you as a parent suspect your child might be involved in drugs, pornography, or you've noticed a drastic change in their personality, investigate; ask questions. If your child has become secretive, withdrawn, or defensive, these are all warnings something might be going on. It's our job as parents to protect our children even from their own self-destruction. There is help for people both with drug addictions and mental illness. It's our hope and desire that people who read this book and are experiencing these same problems will seek out help before they too must stand beside the grave of a child. As a parent, please do not say, "This will not happen to us."

WHEN BAD THINGS
HAPPEN TO GOOD PEOPLE

At one time or another, every person experiences difficulties in their lives: a child born with abnormalities or a family member contracting some life-threatening disease. Yes, problems and difficulties and tragedies are going to come our way. During these trying times, even though we are people of faith, there just seems to be no answer or no reason why these things are happening. We begin questioning God for understanding. Perhaps the question should not be "Why do bad things happen to good people?" but When bad things happen to good people. Bad things are going to happen, for that is a given in life. It's just part of living. There are many things all parents must deal with in raising children. Some of them we can deal with and others we cannot. However, when they do come, we then must be able to cope with them and deal with each situation. When bad things happen, what are we going to do? How are we going to react?

People who love and serve God often cry out at God when their pain becomes hard to bear. When this happens, the God we love and serve understands, listens, and is compassionate and will forgive us when we cry out. Mary and Martha, over the death of their brother, Lazarus, had many questions, and Jesus listened patiently.

> Then Martha, as soon as she heard that Jesus was coming, went and met him: but Mary sat still in the house. Then said Martha unto Jesus, Lord, if thou hadst been here, my brother had not died. Then when Mary was come where Jesus was, and saw him, she fell down at his feet, saying unto him, Lord, if thou hadst been here, my brother had not died.
>
> John 11:20-21 (KJV)

The reaction of Jesus was: When he saw her weeping, and the Jews also weeping which came with her, he groaned in the spirit, and was troubled. And said, Where have ye laid him? They said unto him, Lord, come and see. Jesus wept.

He understood their agony then, just as he understands the agony we go through now. As Christians, we found ourselves coming seeking comfort more and more through our faith. In the end, it was our faith that would carry us through the dark days.

As you continue to read this book, you must understand, as I finally came to realize, bad things are going to happen. It is just a matter of when. And when they do happen, how are we going to react?

When bad things come our way, every one of us handles them differently. We might first deny it has ever happened. This is only a dream, and I'm going to wake up in the morning, and everything is going to be fine.

The rainbow was placed in the sky, reminding us of God's promise that he would never destroy the earth again with water. Every time we see the rainbow, we remember the promises of God for they are sure and faithful never to be broken. God has promised he will never place upon us more than we can bear.

1 Corinthians 10:13 (KJV), "There hath no temptation taken you but such as is common to man: but God is faithful, who will not suffer you to be tempted above that ye are able; but will with the temptation also make a way to escape, that ye may be able to bear it."

This is his promise. Even as people of faith, knowing God is faithful and keeps his promises, we still struggle, crying, "Why?"

There are many joys to experience in life, but sometimes, tragedy follows joy. When children come into our lives, there is such joy and our lives are changed forever. God sends us blessings, and we do not always take advantage of them. Our family experienced, as all do, the ups and downs, the good and bad, the joy and the sadness. When the bad times came, we dealt with each situation differently. That's the way life is.

I performed the wedding of a couple who had separated due to the husband having returned from Vietnam with war-related mental problems. Before they divorced, three children were born, two of which were twins, Carla and Darla. Darla's birth was normal, but Carla had the umbilical cord wrapped around her neck, destroying brain tissue, which left her severely retarded, never progressing beyond the baby stage. Carla died this past May at the age of thirty-four years old. She was cared for so lovingly by parents who did not see the child with retardation, but a beautiful baby who they have nurtured and cared for all those years. This is why Carla lived this long even though doctors said she would not live to see adulthood. I have watched them take care of her over the years.

He and his wife never saw her as a burden but rather a gift from God who taught them so much. They had the attitude, "We cannot change what has happened, so we will turn adversity into something good and positive." It was my joy to perform their wedding, reuniting a couple that so much needed one another; perhaps even more importantly, a child who needed both parents so desperately. It has been twenty-three years since they remarried. They have given their lives caring for a child who many would have considered a burden.

My foster grandmother, Clara Marshal, died at the age of one hundred. As a foster parent, she raised over two hundred children, giving her entire life to the caring of homeless children. My mother was one of her foster children. A baby was placed in her care by the state of Alabama, a baby no one wanted, who was born with severe retardation and never progressed beyond the diaper stage. She cared for him all of his life, loved him, and provided for him the things he needed. Never seen was a severely retarded child, but rather a child sent from God who changed her life and all who knew him. She cared for him into her eighties, until one day, the state came and told her because of her age, they were going to place him in a nursing home. Darrell died having lived to see adulthood, grieving for the only person he knew. He only lived a short time after he was separated from the only person he knew.

Yes, we all can learn from others who have experienced the challenges of life. When we look at the challenges many face, our challenges seem to be so small, and yet, we cry, "Oh, God, why me?"

Our challenge was not a child with severe retardation but rather with internal problems no one could see visibly, such as mental illness and drug addiction that followed him into adulthood. Often we see these as problems the person themselves must work out because as adults who must take on responsibilities.

The bad things that happen can turn into joy if we will allow God to work in our lives through them. Tragedy is going to come in our lives in some form or fashion. The question is, how are we going to handle the things that come? We can blame God, the doctors, and the society in which we live. We can always find someone to blame, someone to pay for bad things that come our way. In the end, we realize this is part of living, and we can use the bad to make us better people.

You might be one to experience the tragedy, devastation, and heartbreak when bad things happen to someone close to you. Perhaps our story can help you prepare when it does strike. In this story, you are going to read of the journey of a young man who was born with mental illness and later became a crack addict.

The hardest thing for Betsy and me as parents was hearing our son being called a "crack head." We were average people with average jobs traveling through life. We attended church every time the doors were open, yet our son was a crack head. People living in the streets are referred to as "crack heads." Not our son. He was raised better than that. Yet it was true; he was a crack head. When we finally admitted Chris was on crack cocaine, we were at lost as to what to do.

How could such a sweet child do all the things that Chris did? Did his journey have to end this way? What could we have done to change the outcome? Finally, what is our government doing to fight a growing problem in our society? These are all questions that will be addressed in this book. Perhaps you will find your family facing some of the same issues. Maybe through our pain, you can find answers.

UNDERSTANDING TRAGEDY AND EXPERIENCING JOY

One cannot understand tragedy until they've experienced joy. You cannot enjoy the springtime if you have not experienced the wintertime. The greatest joy of my life came the day I met Betsy. Each one of us remembers the day we met our partner for life. Perhaps you even knew the moment you laid eyes on him or her that that person was going to be your wife or husband. What was it that caught your eye? Was it the beauty or the personality? Whatever it was, it was special. The joyous times we all have experienced with our children began the day we first met and thought, One day, this person will be my mate. The first time I met Betsy was sitting in church. She did not know, nor did I, how our lives were going to be changed. Her, sitting there looking so beautiful, and me, what did I have to offer? I could not take my eyes off her and felt myself being distracted from worship. Returning my attention back to worship, I remember thinking that I had to meet her.

I had just recently gone through a divorce. My wife had abandoned me, leaving me with two beautiful children. I was lonely and needed someone to talk to. Somehow, I knew Betsy and I would get together. I just did not know when. Who would want someone like me? I was skinny with red hair and had a big car that looked like a tank. I later joked with Betsy that she married me for my car. It could not have been for my money; I had none. All I had was a Dodge Monaco and two of the sweetest children one could ever have. They were the joy of my heart. How could I get her to go out with me?

Our journey began on a Saturday night in the winter of 1971 in the home of my sister, Sharon, and her husband, Jack. Jack baptized Betsy and started me on my preaching career. It was not uncommon for Jack and Sharon to have fellowships at their house. They were always having the church over, and over forty-two years later, they still entertain many people. They lived in a mobile home on Hunter Loop Road outside of Montgomery, a mobile home they would later sell to Betsy and me, I am sure, at great loss. There were a lot of young people from church at the party. We all had a good time. The plan was I was to take Betsy home after the party. We left around ten and just rode around talking. We hit it off and talked about what we wanted from life. She was smart, a senior, and wanted to go to college. I had already traveled to several countries and served two tours in the Vietnam War. I came home on a hardship to take custody of my two children.

Our romance blossomed. I was like some lovesick teenager who could not stay away, so I spent a lot of time at her house pestering her and her mother. We were married a year later in the office of the probate judge of Butler County, Alabama. I had little to offer. What a way to start. I suppose some have started off with far less. We had $5 in quarters Mama gave us on the day we got married. Stopping at McDonald's on Fairview Avenue in Montgomery, we shared our new life together over a hamburger, fries, and Coke. The first night, we stayed at my sister's house in north Montgomery. We had no money and nowhere else to go. There was no money for a honeymoon. Soon after, we moved into an apartment my grandmother had at her house. The important thing was I had me a big car, and some said that's what did it. Betsy had to get her own car after we married—a 1968 Chevy for $800. Mama cosigned with her to get it. I drove a truck for a grocery company out of Montgomery making $125 a week and with no money in the bank.

Betsy and I married when she was seventeen years old. She was the bright spot in my life when there had been many dark clouds and storms. Thirty-eight years later, I cannot imagine life without her. I never dreamed I would find anyone, and along came this beautiful high school beauty queen. I remember exactly where we were when she said, "I think I love you." "Think!" I suppose she is still thinking thirty-eight years later having raised five children, two that she inherited from a previous marriage. I sometimes remind her of those words, "I think I love you." We laugh, and she says, "I'm still thinking."

From the beginning, David and Jim loved Betsy, and she loved them as though they were her own children. Life was good, even though we experienced struggles along the way, but we were happy, and both of us worked very hard to make the marriage work. We had few problems with one another or with David and Jim. This was truly a marriage made in heaven.

We moved into a house in the Oak Park section of Montgomery on West Street—our first house. We both worked for a pest control company, making $750 a month between us. We were happy and would later move back to Pintlala into a mobile home living on the Brady homeplace.

Life was good. David and Jim were sweet boys and never gave us problems. God blessed our marriage when I landed a job working for the United States Air Force. It would take me all over the world until I retired after over thirty years of service.

My father loved Betsy almost as much as I did. From the first moment I brought her home to meet him and mom, they just connected. My dad always came up with a name for everyone. Each one of us eleven children had some form of nickname he had given us. Nothing was different when he met Betsy. I do not know why he gave her the name he did. Her new name was "Ma Chubby." I did not consider her to be chubby. She was just beautiful, and I was lucky to have her. A coworker many years later would ask me, "How did you get such a beautiful wife?" My reply to him was, "Some of us have it, and some of us don't." What a blessing she has been in my life and still is.

As much as Betsy loved David and Jim, she desired to have a child of her own. Expectant parents will sometime fantasize about having a child. They imagine the life they will share together. Parents dream of having someone whom they can love unconditionally and who will love and need them. This capacity to love and a fierce need to protect is as natural as getting up in the morning. It does not stop after a child leaves the nest but will always continue, just in a different way. Protecting their children is something God-given and never ceases just because the child leaves home in search of their own way. Parents take on many different roles: doctor, counselor, and advisor.

Children provide a sense of purpose for parents and become an integral part of the parents' lives, and when something happens to alter the purpose, the consequences can be devastating. The greatest fear of most parents is having a child die, as they cannot imagine being able to emotionally cope with such a loss. When a couple is trying to have a child, it's never considered this child will be anything but normal. Nor does one even entertain the notion this child might die. Not considered is whether their child will have some form of mental retardation or be born with some other affliction.

Over the next few years, we tried to have children, but Betsy continued to have miscarriages, even having a tubal pregnancy that led to surgery. This lowered the possibility of her getting pregnant. We had a wonderful gynecologist who knew that she would make a good mother. This was already proven by her care for two children she did not give birth to but loved from the day she first met them.

Jim was just a little guy, one year old, and David was almost three. They took to her, as we say down South, "like flies take to syrup" or "ants to sugar." She was a wonderful mother, even at seventeen years old, and was mature far beyond her years. But she always longed for a child from her own womb. As I have said, she could not have loved any child more than she loved David and Jim, but there was that longing. Her doctor worked very closely with her to try to find the answer and did everything medical science could offer to help her find why she could not have children.

I remembered the story from the Old Testament in the book of 1 Samuel: the story of Hannah, who could not have children. She prayed to God that he would open her womb, and if he would give her a child, she would give him to God all the days of his life. We prayed for a child, and every day, we would pray the same prayer over and over again. How many other women desire to have children? They watch others have them, and yet, their womb was closed for some reason or another. It seemed it was not for them to have children. Through faith, we turned it over to God. Whatever God's will was, we would live with it.

When Betsy made an appointment with her doctor, I was not even aware she was even thinking she might be pregnant.

I opened the front door of the house as she was running toward me, returning from her appointment. She was waving a little book the doctor had given her about how one should conduct themselves while pregnant and what to expect during the pregnancy. She was shouting, "We're going to have a baby! We're going to have a baby!" She was crying. I grabbed her, and we began to hug and kiss. About this time, David and Jim, who were just little guys, came running out to see what all the commotion was about. We told them they were going to have a little brother or sister in about seven and a half months. There was a celebration around the Brady house that night. We celebrated by gathering around the fireplace and talking about the new baby who was going to come our way. It had been almost five years since we had been married, and now what we had talked about, prayed about, and dreamed about was going to happen. We prayed she would not have another miscarriage. Betsy did everything right to make sure she was able to carry the child to term.

Everything pointed out to be a normal pregnancy, with the morning sickness and the craving for crazy things. Time began to draw near, so it was important for me to make sure I had the car gassed up, for we lived twenty-five miles from Montgomery and wanted to be ready.

If anybody enjoyed being pregnant, it was Betsy Beck Brady. She was always smiling and laughing and carrying on, preparing for the day we would bring this little one home. All expectant parents react this way, with happiness and joy. Preparing a new bedroom, buying a baby bed, and all the things the new baby will need.

We talked about what to name him or her. At that time, you had to wait to find out the sex of your child. I always thought it would be a girl, and so I went to the store and purchased a dress and prepared for a girl. I did this again when Mike and Ricky were born, thinking, This time, it has to be a girl. Betsy always said it was going to be a boy. She was listening to her mother, who would say, "If you carry the baby low, it will be a boy, and if you carry the baby high, it will be a girl." I do not remember if she carried high or low, but she would say, "You should just as well get ready. It's going to be a boy." My reply was, "As long as the baby is healthy, that's all that matters. But here is the dress, just in case." It turned out she was right, and I was wrong. This did not matter. We were excited, for a bundle of joy was about to come and change our lives forever.

On September 14, 1976, Christopher Michael Brady came into the world at eight pounds, two ounces, and twenty-two inches long. He was about the prettiest baby I had ever seen. All parents say their child is beautiful. All my boys were handsome and had no problems attracting the girls. I went to the hospital and stood in front of the observation window looking at him, waiting for the day I would be able to hold him. Betsy's doctor's partner came into the room to discuss with her what she needed to do as she prepared to carry our son home.

Three days later we departed the hospital and arrived at our house in Grady with Betsy's mother and others there waiting to see and hold our beautiful baby. David and Jim were standing on the steps with great expectations, waiting to see their new brother. Those first few days after we arrived home, all Betsy did was hold Chris, with David and Jim taking turns. It was a happy time for us all.

My mother wrote many poems over the course of her eighty-seven years. Several are recorded in this book. Of all the poems she wrote, I believe the one included here best describes how all parents feel when a baby is brought into their lives.

A Gift of Love

An angel paid a visit
To our house in the night
And left a small bundle
Of heaven's delight:

A precious little baby,
From his head to his toes.
And filled with a mischief
Only a small child knows.

A splash of bright color
From the pot in the skies.
He sent you to us,
The perfect part of paradise.

No greater gift from God
Could he send down to earth
Than the proof of his love,
The great miracle of birth.

No portrait on canvas
Could be equaled by man.
For this was created
By a Master's hand.

Life's Memories, Thelma Brady (page 47)

Storms that might be brewing down the road do not cross your
mind when a new child arrives. A parent does not consider that
this beautiful baby, this gift from God, will someday experience
terrible and agonizing tragedy. This moment in life is special, and
all a new mom and dad see is how wonderful life is. Everything

you do, your every thought, your every action is how you will go about protecting and caring for this gift from God.

No one would have guessed the agony and the turmoil we as a family would go through during the next twenty-nine years. We watched him take his first step and say his first word. The first birthday arrives and in the moment of joy, there was no thought we would have to endure the frustrations that would come along with mental illness and drug addiction.

There were many wonderful times during those years, but the sun disappeared behind the clouds and turned into a storm quickly. However, the sun always emerged, sometimes leaving us exhausted. After a period of time, life returned to normal until the next storm came. As Chris grew older, the storms came more frequently, and so did the ability to withstand them.

He was our son and always would be. We would never abandon him nor cast him aside. We always were there for him when difficult times arose. Do not think just because a child has mental illness or even a drug addiction that we did not experience joy. There were many times of joy; however, nothing prepared us for that what was to come.

Chris's early years were normal. What a great time it was. From early on, Chris was a good baby. He rarely cried, only when he was hungry or needed a diaper change. David and Jim loved caring for their new brother and never did show any signs of jealousy. In church, everyone wanted to hold him. We were so proud of him. We took him to church the very next Sunday after he came home from the hospital. Yes, life was good.

On September 30, 1977, God blessed our family with Jonathan Michael, who was born a little over a year after Chris. On February 28, 1979, along came little Richard Allen, the smallest of the three born to Betsy and me. Ricky would later become the largest of our five children, with an even bigger heart. We decided that five was the magic number, and it was not for us to have a girl. It was time to quit having babies and get on with the business of raising our family. Our doctor would say, "Try for a girl." Our reply was, "The odds are not in our favor."

When Chris was two years old, we could tell he was a smart child but had a short attention span, which is a symptom of several things, ADD being one of them. We did not think a lot about it. He was normal in every way and was a joy. He loved riding on the handle bars of the plow when I worked the garden. I let him ride back and forth. He would always say, "Again, Daddy. Again, Daddy." So he partnered with me in plowing the garden.

He showed all the signs of being a normal four-year-old. All five boys were doing well and got along well together. They fought little and seemed to enjoy one another. Chris began kindergarten and did well. There were no serious behavior problems. He did the things children do as they grow up. His one big problem as a child, and probably the worst, was his temper tantrums. We never saw that as sign of a problem childhood. Many children have temper tantrums, especially if they discover that it's how to get their way. Chris also liked hiding from us. While living in Greensboro, Alabama, Chris often ran off and could not be found. One particular time, we had searched high and low for him in a panic. I was running up and down the road looking for him while Betsy went the other way. We ran back to the house only to discover him hiding behind the couch. He never moved in all that time. I wanted to whip him but could not. I should have punished him but was too happy to find him. He learned at an early age what he could get away with and what he could not. He could also turn on the charm. He never, in all his years, lost that ability. Everyone would say how sweet he was and comment about his manners. All of our children exhibited good manners everywhere they went. We received kind remarks from people who would say, "Your children are so well-mannered." Chris was charming and handsome, and he knew it.

As I look back on it, I see a child whose mind was always racing for attention. The best way to handle this is to ignore the child, or so we thought. That's like trying to ignore a noise that won't stop or a horn that will not quit blowing.

At the first sign of trouble or a sign that something is not right, parents should start asking questions. It might be only a minor thing such as temper tantrums; however, minor things turn into major situations that are not easily remedied. For example, ignoring a child's crying by saying, "It's a way to get attention." Never ignore a child's smallest problems, for as we learned, a small breeze can turn into a storm very quickly.

WITH CLOUDS
COME STORMS

I do not remember when Chris first began to experience problems. We noticed he was somewhat different than the other boys. For example, he was very difficult to discipline. As a small child, he would become angry over very small things, but he was not mean to us or his brothers. These were concerns that we wrote off as growing up. We learned the hard way it was not just part of growing up. There were problems. Mental illness is something one is born with. It's in genetics. Children inherit a lot of things from their parents: hair color, facial features, height, and a disposition to do certain things or follow a particular occupation. As children inherit good things, they also inherit the bad. Out of our five children, two are bipolar, and two have attention deficit disorder. This was not found out until many years after they were born. It is important to have children tested early on. By doing this, one can eliminate certain future problems. If they are not diagnosed correctly, they cannot be given the proper help. Jim was diagnosed as having a learning disorder later determined to be ADD. Because of the wrong diagnosis, he was put in special education classes he did not need to be in. We insisted on having him retested, finding out we were correct. He went on to graduate from high school and then graduated from Faulkner University in Montgomery with a degree in business administration. Ricky finished high school and began working for a power company and now owns a very lucrative landscaping business. Mike has a brilliant mind and can design a yard into a picture perfect landscape. He can build almost anything and has always worked with his hands. He has a daily struggle with bipolar disorder and must take medication.

When a family begins to face challenges with a child, time becomes an important factor. Understand, bipolar disorder is very difficult to diagnose. In small children, it often is misdiagnosed.

Mental illness need not destroy families, if treated. Left untreated, it can have devastating consequences, as we have seen in the life of our son. Even after his death, we did not understand it, so I began to do some research. I found there were many Web sites on the internet that were very helpful with the situation we were in with our son. The following site, www.NAMI.org, had a lot of helpful information.

What is Mental Illness:

Mental illnesses are medical conditions that disrupt a person's thinking, feeling, mood, ability to relate to others and daily functioning. Just as diabetes is a disorder of the pancreas, mental illnesses are medical conditions that often result in a diminished capacity for coping with the ordinary demands of life. Mental illnesses can affect people of any age, race, religion, or income. Mental illnesses are not the result of personal weakness, lack of character, or poor upbringing. Mental illnesses are treatable. Most people diagnosed with a serious mental illness can experience relief from their symptoms by actively participating in an individual treatment plan.

Even though mental illness is widespread in the population, the main burden of illness is concentrated in a much smaller proportion—about 6 percent, or 1 in 17 Americans—who live with a serious mental illness. The National Institute of Mental Health reports that one in four adults—approximately 57.7 million Americans—experience a mental health disorder in a given year. The U.S. Surgeon General reports that 10 percent of children and adolescents in the United States suffer from serious emotional and mental disorders that cause significant functional impairment in their day-to-day lives at home, in school and with peers. The World Health Organization has reported that four of the 10 leading causes of disability in the U.S. and other developed countries are mental disorders. By 2020, Major Depressive illness will be the leading cause of disability in the world for women and children.

Mental illness usually strike individuals in the prime of their lives, often during adolescence and young adulthood. All ages are susceptible, but the young and the old are especially vulnerable. Without treatment the consequences of mental illness for the individual and society are staggering: unnecessary disability, unemployment, substance abuse, homelessness, inappropriate incarceration, suicide and wasted lives; The economic cost of untreated mental illness is more than 100 billion dollars each year in the United States. The best treatments for serious mental illnesses today are highly effective; between 70 and 90 percent of individuals have significant reduction of symptoms and improved quality of life with a combination of pharmacological and psychosocial treatments and supports. With appropriate effective medication and a wide range of services tailored to their needs, most people who live with serious mental illnesses can significantly reduce the impact of their illness and find a satisfying measure of achievement and independence. A key concept is to develop expertise in developing strategies to manage the illness process.

As time went on, I began to think that Chris was going to be fine. He did not seem to have any abnormalities in his life like some of the things we just mentioned in the preceding paragraph. But as Chris grew older, we discovered how true they were.

Betsy and I moved our family to Alexander City, Alabama, to become directors and house parents of the James Cullin's Children's Home. Everyone was excited because this was a new adventure. Our oldest son met his wife, Jenny, there. They have three wonderful children. Jim began dating a young lady from Dublin, Alabama, whom he married. They have two beautiful daughters. Yes, life was good, and we were happy working as a director of the children's home and as youth minister and associate minister.

My full-time job was with the United States Air Force Reserve, working as a crew chief on a C-130 Hercules airplane. There was much to do, and we stayed busy. We had a wonderful church family, children who were doing well, and we were making a difference in the lives of other children. There were no signs of an approaching storm. There were small clouds but nothing we considered would suggest a serious, life-changing storm.

We served in Alexander City, working there for four years and enjoying a good ministry impacting the lives of many children. There were some signs Chris was having difficulties but nothing to suggest anything bad. He learned to play the trombone in the local junior high school band. He flourished in school and was popular. Chris enjoyed playing baseball on the local Dixie Youth team. It was there he had his first girlfriend, or what he thought was his girlfriend. He seemed to be maturing, and there was no reason to believe he would not. There were some small behavioral issues, but we thought he was just a little more difficult than the other children. Nothing we could not handle.

In 1990, Betsy and I decided to return to Pintlala, Alabama, to the community where I grew up to build a house. The storm clouds began to build, and as Chris turned thirteen years old, our first real storm hit with tremendous force. The problems began to mount as he became uncontrollable.

First, there were serious anger problems and difficulty in getting him to get up out of the bed in the morning. It was always a fight to get him up. When we finally succeeded, he would be extremely angry. Discipline was a problem. We could not restrict him for punishment. To restrict him was a confinement sentence. His anger increased, even over small offenses. One afternoon, Chris came in and asked if he could drive the car to the store. I had taught him, as I did all of our children, how to drive by sitting in my lap. They would steer the car down the driveway or around the parking lot. I then let them sit by themselves as they became big enough, teaching them how to operate the car. This was something I thought was a good thing to do. It was also a lot of fun. Even to this day, when we turn into our driveway, if some of the grandchildren are in the car, they will say, "Granddaddy, can I drive?" I will allow them to crawl into my lap and steer to the house, and as we come to a stop, they blow the horn.

With Chris, this was seen as a license to take the car, so we had to hide the car keys. On this day, he came in and said, "I want to use the car." My response was, "Absolutely not. You are not old enough to drive on the highway." He began to tell me, "I know how to drive, and I'm going to take the car." There was no arguing nor reasoning with him. His demands began to get out of control, and he threw the telephone. To this day, there are marks within our house where a bat made a hole. The front door was broken down the middle from being slammed so hard. Furniture was broken, dishes were thrown, and much was destroyed. We did not know what to do. His two older brothers were out of the nest. David was attending school at Auburn University, living most of the time in Alexander City. Jim was working full-time and had his own small apartment.

We thought, How could any child do what he does, say what he says, and treat people he loves in such a manner? We even wondered how we could commit him, but we never seriously considered this option until much later.

One day, there was a confrontation between us. I was fed up. I thought, I'm in charge. I'm the one in authority here. He's going to listen to me, and as long as he lives in this house, he's going to do what I say. I had made up my mind. He was not going to rule the house anymore. I was going to take it back. When I came in from work one afternoon, there was an immediate confrontation. Chris was as big as me and very strong. I pushed him up against the refrigerator and told him he was not going to talk to me that way. Everyone was upset. I just walked out of the house to cool off. He went up to his room, and that was all for that night, but that was not the end of it.

He went to school the next day and told the teacher I beat him up while his brothers held him. His brothers were small and could never have done this. The teacher did what was right. When child abuse is suspected in the home, they are to call the Department of Human Services. We were turned in for suspected child abuse. We received a letter in the mail that stated we should bring Chris in for consultation to the Department of Human Services. Not knowing what was going on, we went. We were informed they had received information that our son was being beaten in the home. She said, "Your son said you beat him while his brothers held him."

I said, "You should see his brothers. They are half his size."

She did not believe this. She believed Chris, for she had already talked with him in private and gotten his side of the story. I knew then what she was talking about.

I said to her, "You are referring to an incident that happened in our house a few weeks ago when there was a confrontation between him and me. His brothers had nothing to do with it. It was between him and me, and I felt he needed to be disciplined. He is only thirteen years old, and he is not going to talk to me and curse his mother and me and get away with it. As for the beating, all I did was push him up against the refrigerator and tell him he was not going to talk to me this way. I never hit him."

She said to me, "Mr. Brady, you should hit him two or three times about his buttocks."

If I had not been so angry and so disgusted, I would've laughed. It was not a laughing matter. I said, "Lady, he is bigger than me." We were warned by this lady of the consequences if we continued to beat him.

There are extreme frustrations when dealing with someone with mental illness. Although they are sick and need help, help oftentimes is far away and even more expensive than a family can pay. Many families, including ours, have been bankrupted by this kind of illness. Good parents have been marked as bad parents because they could not control a mentally ill child. For a long time, Betsy and I could not talk about the possibility of Chris being sick. We always thought he was going to get better. He was going to grow out of it. We just had to be more patient. But our patience wore thin to the point of breaking down. Unfortunately, during these very tumultuous times, my job required me to fly with the United States Air Force Reserve to distant locations. To make matters worse, I had to go to the Gulf War in 1990.

UNDERSTANDING
MENTAL ILLNESS

I came from a very poor family, being the middle child of eleven children. Because of this, our family had some hard times; at least, they were hard compared to this day and time. The youth today have many more temptations than we did in the fifties and sixties. With no TV, no telephone, no car, and no Internet, we filled our time with other things, like talking to one another, fishing, and making our own entertainment.

Perhaps in our efforts to make sure our children have more, we gave them too much. This was not the reason for Chris's drug problem, nor do I believe it to be the reason some of us fail as parents. I believe Chris was doomed from the day he was born. Why do I say this? Not because we were bad parents. Not because there was a lack of love or a lack of attention given to him. He received the same attention and the same opportunities our other children received. I truly believe it was our inability to recognize Chris was mentally ill, even at an early age. The signs were there. We did not know what they were. My grandfather was mentally ill. I have sisters and brothers who have fought the battle of mental illness all their life. To many people, mental illness is only words. Some of those words are bipolar and manic depressant. Some are worse than others. Mental illness caused my nephew to take his life at the youthful age of twenty-seven. When did we as parents recognize Chris had a problem, and why were we unable to do anything about it?

One day, Chris became very angry with his brother and began to chase him. He chased him into my car, where his brother locked the door. Chris took his fist and broke the window of the car. I made him come into the house and sit down. The anger left as fast as it came. We tried to decide what to do. I thought about calling the sheriff's department but finally ruled that out. It was one of those times we did not know what to do. We had never experienced this before, but we knew, at that very moment, there was a problem. We just did not know what.

We looked in the yellow pages and tried to find somewhere to start. We began with the mental health department. Over the next several weeks, Chris received counseling on how to manage anger, but it did little good. He became angry over small things. We were referred to an in-house program in Dothan, Alabama. The cost was astronomical. Knowing we could not afford this kind of care but having good insurance that paid a good portion, we worked out a deal with this organization. They agreed to accept insurance consignment. We were able to get him admitted, but Chris was slick. He could manipulate the system and would tell people what he knew they wanted to hear. Betsy and I traveled the one hundred miles every week to sit in the counseling sessions and try to help in the healing process. The counselor told me, "Chris is not ready to go home yet but has made tremendous progress doing everything we ask of him. If he continues to make this kind of progress, I believe he will be able to return home soon." I told the counselor, "Chris is using this system and will tell you anything you want to hear." I do not believe the counselor understood everything I was saying. I wish I could say they did him some good. All the money was not wasted. We were soon to learn just how right I was. He had convinced them he was a good boy and had learned his lesson and wanted to go home. The counselors were convinced he was better and understood what his responsibilities were and how to manage his anger. After twenty-one days, he returned home.

After Chris returned home, we tried to be patient doing things together. We encouraged him in school, but his grades were not good. His teacher said he was very intelligent but just did not try and would not listen. They would say, "It's like he doesn't want to be here. He just wants to be with his friends."

I would insist he do certain chores along with the other boys, but it was difficult, and he would only do them halfway. Time went on, and we wrestled with it. Every day was a day he would need to be disciplined. We, like many parents, refused to believe there was nothing here but an unruly child. Mental illness never crossed our minds.

Up to this time, Chris had not been diagnosed with any form of mental illness, just with an anger problem. "He needs to learn how to vent his anger," the experts would tell us. Vent his anger, I thought, what a joke. We would just sit and look at one another while his mother went about preparing our meal. I would make him sit, regardless of how mad he would get.

Did the community, the church, the school, or even other parts of our family know there were problems? Not all of it. They knew there were some problems in discipline. Betsy and I hid it for a long time because we were at first embarrassed. We also did not want to admit there was a major problem within our family.

We tried not to fuss when someone came to the house. We put on an "Everything is fine. Everybody is happy," attitude. We got up one Sunday morning, as any other morning, and there was a confrontation of some kind. This started the day off with a knot in our stomachs. Sometimes we did not have the desire to go to the church building to worship. How could we worship when our life was falling apart? This made it difficult to put on a smile like everything was fine and life was good. But we had to put on the show so no one would know we had a problem. There were good days when he would do well, and we would laugh and joke. Betsy and I tried to focus on the good times and kept his mind off confrontational things.

With mental illness, all the family is affected. His siblings were affected by hearing vulgar language and the way he treated those who loved him the most. Mental illness affects everybody around the individual. It is not until it is diagnosed and treated that an individual can live a normal life. The treatment becomes a lifetime venture. One cannot turn mental illness off like water from a faucet. It is not something you can sweep under the rug. It will eventually come out, and then everyone will know.

You Are Good Parents

After learning of the situation within our family, one of my coworkers, who was very close to me, said, "Larry, you and Betsy are good people. You are good parents. You are the same parents that raised the other four boys."

Proverbs 22:6 (KJV) has been used to mislead good parents: "Train a child up in the way he should go and when he is old he will not depart from it." How many times have we read that scripture? Betsy always had a different view on this scripture, saying, "I cannot believe God will hold parents responsible for what their adult children do." Talking with fellow preachers, seeking advice about Chris, some of them even said, "He needs to have a closer relationship with God."

In John 9:1-12 (KJV), we read about a man born blind. The people began to ask Jesus about the man's blindness and how he came to be blind. "Who was it that sinned to cause the blindness, him or His parents?" Many religious leaders feel people are experiencing these kinds of situations because they are sinners. All one needs to do is correct their life. If they just correct their life, everything is going to be fine. Who sinned to make our son do the things he did?

A study by Baylor University found:

> Clergy often deny or dismiss the existence of mental illness. In a study published in Mental Health, Religion and Culture, researchers found that in a study of 293 Christian church members, more than 32 percent were told by their churches preacher they or their loved one did not really have a mental illness. The study found these church members were told the cause of their problem was solely spiritual in nature, such as a personal sin, lack of faith or demonic involvement. Baylor researchers also found that women were more likely than men to have their mental disorders dismissed by the church. All of the participants in both studies were previously diagnosed by a licensed mental health provider as having a serious mental illness, like bipolar disorder and schizophrenia, prior to approaching their local church for assistance.

In the past, people who had mental illnesses or were considered to have some type of abnormality in their life would be locked away in some mental institution. This was done so society could be protected. Parents even tied their children to chairs and to the bed simply because they did not understand this disease. Children who were unruly would be locked away, some for life.

With more Bible study and stronger faith, some religious leaders feel everything can be taken care of. A parent often says, "I must have made a mess out of my training. I'll just have to try harder. I will be a better Christian, making me be a better parent." On and on the cycle goes until one day, we come to understand that it has nothing to do with parenting. I am not a bad person, and I have not mistreated my family.

Attending a revival, I heard a sermon on Proverbs 22:6. Like many others of faith, I have read this scripture many times. Usually, like others, I would take it literally to mean, "If your child did not turn out right, then you, somewhere and somehow, failed in your responsibilities as a parent. You were not a good parent; therefore, repentance must be forthcoming." I had always understood it this way. Betsy never did, even before we had difficulties with Chris, take this position. She would always say, "There has to be another meaning. When children get away from home, out from under our influence, why should we be to blame?" I listened attentively as the preacher spoke on this subject. He said, "The book of Proverbs speaks in proverbs, and they are generally true, but not always." This sermon did a lot to help me understand some things I had been missing. In short, he said, "There are a lot of good parents who are suffering unnecessarily. They think themselves to be bad parents simply because their children did not turn out the way they wanted them to." Until this night, I had never had a clear understanding of this verse. The speaker talked about parents who were God-fearing Christian people but were wrestling with the fact their child had turned out badly and they were to blame.

This book is about how we as parents can come to understand that mental illness is not something done to our children. It's not something within our control. It's about a family that struggled every day, trying to do what was right and trying to bring their children up in the way that God wanted them to. But ultimately, in the end, it made no difference. Betsy and I were not bad parents. This sermon helped me change my attitude toward the rearing of children. It is true that when children are trained in the way of the Lord, the likelihood of them turning out to be God-fearing Christian people increases a hundredfold. When children see parents making a demonstration of Christ in their lives every day, it does have an impact upon them.

How many people have stood in the midst of the debris of a life storm trying to struggle with their feelings and trying to make some sense of all of it? Those in the religious community often cry out about faith at times like this. "Where is your faith?" they ask. After Chris's death, one lady responded by asking me about my faith. Perhaps she was quoting Jesus when he asked the disciples about their faith, but those were different circumstances altogether.

As parents, we came to understand it wasn't our fault. There is so much guilt that causes anxiety and anger. This can lead to problems in the marriage and sometimes divorce.

We finally took Chris to our family doctor and just opened up to him about what was going on. We did not know what to do. We were searching for some direction. He asked us, after listening very patiently, "Have you considered the possibility that Chris might be mentally ill?"

Mentally ill! I thought he might be saying our son was crazy, because this was how so many people think about it. Twenty years ago, if it was determined one had mental illness, there was a stigma attached to it. One person said to me, "Don't use the words mental illness. Use some other word that doesn't sound as bad." The more we read and learned, the more we came to understand mental illness can be treated.

Mental illness does not mean a person is crazy. It does mean it needs to be treated. If a person does not receive treatment, the consequences can be devastating. Everyday living becomes a problem.

We did not discuss with any of our extended family about Chris's mental disease; however, at this point in his life, he had not even been diagnosed as being mentally ill. Mental illness is a stigma people don't like to talk about. Even after discussing this with our family doctor, we did not believe it ourselves. The things he talked about happened to others. We did not understand what we were dealing with. The doctor gave us material so we might better understand, but it did little to help us in the coping process.

Chris received medication, but it was difficult to get him to take it. He said, "I am not crazy." In his way of thinking, taking medicine would mean he was. We did notice while on the medication that he did better. He was calmer and more controllable and did better at school. While taking this kind of medication, one cannot waver in treatment. It has to be taken constantly to be effective. Also, there are other side effects when one does not take the medication regularly.

Things seemed to be getting better, and we were doing everything that a normal family does. I coached Little League softball and baseball and spent a lot of time with my children. It seemed like we had found the answer, but it would not last. Mental illness is for life and does not go away. It is not outgrown like growing pains. It is a disease for life, and one must learn to cope.

No Fear

While living in Hollins, Alabama, Chris made friends with one of the teenagers from the community. They went everywhere together and did many things together, and even after we moved from that community, they stayed friends. We will call him "Jack." At some point, Chris and Jack decided they did not want to live at home anymore and decided to run away. They discussed where they were going to go, according to the account given by Chris later. They talked about how they were going to go and where the money would come from for this adventure. Chris was fourteen years old and knew how to drive, and drive he did. He stole the keys to my Ford Escort and departed, putting his plan into action. He left very early in the morning and drove the eighty miles north to the school where Jack was attending. Jack was fifteen years old and had a learner's permit to drive. This would come to be an asset for them as they traveled, for Jack did most of the driving. Chris went to the school, having already made an arrangement with his friend to meet at a certain time outside the school grounds. They traveled back to Jack's house, where he stole $1,800 that his parents had locked up for the family business. Having packed the car with different types of camping materials, they headed out for the North Carolina mountains.

After we discovered Chris had run away and the car was gone, I immediately called the sheriff's department. With a good description of the car and the direction we felt it was headed, we were assured by the sheriff's department, "Mr. Brady, if your son puts that little red car on the road, he won't get far." It turned out to be a joke. Not saying that efforts were not made, but the joke was on us, because these two teenagers drove that little red car 2,800 miles.

The next eight days were a nightmare, and had it not been for some very close Christian friends, I do not believe we could have survived. We needed to look for them but did not have the financial resources. We were prepared to head for the mountains to look for them, for we were positive that was where they were going. We were right, but they never arrived because they got lost. My friend said to me, "I know you feel you need to go look, but I do not believe you are going to be successful. We understand you need to go." This friend offered me a credit card to take with me for expenses, but I would not take it.

Jack's parents went one way, and we went the other, hoping to make up a lot of ground. It did not seem the police investigation was going anywhere, and they had no leads as to where the two children might have gone. Betsy cried buckets of tears. It did not matter about all of the terrible things we were enduring and had endured. All that mattered was that Chris was out there somewhere, perhaps hurt.

We loaded our van and headed for North Carolina, not knowing what we would find or if we would find anything. All we knew was we had to try. We went first to the Nantahala River, where we had been white-water rafting with our family and youth group from church. When Chris and Jack departed Clay County, Alabama, they traveled I-20 toward Atlanta, but even for a seasoned driver, Atlanta can be very scary. They knew they were to take I-75 toward Chattanooga but evidently got confused and headed south toward Florida. They did not recognize their mistake until they saw the Florida state line. They turned around and got on I-95, which travels the East Coast. They stayed on I-95 until they came into North Carolina. Jack was lonely and wanted to talk to his girlfriend, so they stopped at a hotel and got a room, and Jack called his girlfriend.

There was a nationwide search for the boys. I wondered as to the intensity of this nationwide search because it seemed they drove wherever they wanted to. Chris told us they even went through checkpoints where the police actually checked Jack's license. They never recognized them as the children they were looking for. While talking to his girlfriend, she informed her mother Jack was on the phone, and a trace was started. His girlfriend was told to keep them talking, giving the police long enough to get over to where they were. During the conversation, the hotel manager knocked on their door and said the police had called and asked if two boys fitting their description were registered at the hotel. He warned the boys for he was afraid he would get in trouble for allowing underage children to register in his hotel. They ran and got in the car, according to Chris, and as they drove out of one end of the parking lot, the police came in the other end. They escaped and continued north on I-95.

In the meantime, Betsy and I were on the other side of the state in the mountains. We had shown the picture of Chris to local establishments in the area, and someone had said that they had seen them or someone who looked like them. This all turned out to be false information. We called the other family, as they were searching the other part of the state, and told them what we had found out. They headed in our direction, but in the meantime, we found out our information was not correct.

We decided to return home because there was nothing else we could do. We were out of money and exhausted both mentally and physically. We got the phone call that they had found them in North Carolina. We were told it would be a matter of minutes and the police would have them in custody, for the police were en route to pick them up and for us not to worry. However, it was not to be. As the boys continued traveling north, they stopped in Virginia and spent some time on the beach. They spent the night camping and having a good time. As they continued north, they saw a sign that said "Manhattan" and decided to take the Manhattan exit, thinking it would be a great adventure and a story to tell. They wound up in a very bad section of town. Lost and not knowing which way to go, a man approached them and asked if they needed help. He led them back over to I-95, where they continued north to Boston, Massachusetts. At this point, they were almost out of money and decided to continue on to Canada, not knowing how far it was. They got as far as Lincoln, New Hampshire, where they ran out of gas. There, they camped out in a park. This was the end of the road. They were eighty miles from the Canadian border. A policeman stopped to find out what they were doing. He told them that they could not camp there. Chris told him they were from Alabama and had run away. They were taken to the local police station, where they were given some food. We finally received a phone call stating that they were in custody. It had been eight days since they had left Clay County, Alabama, and had traveled over 2,800 miles.

With the help of friends from church, an airline ticket was purchased for me to fly to Manchester, New Hampshire, and then I drove the eighty miles from there to pick up my car. I returned to Manchester, where the boys were in a halfway house waiting for us to come and get them. The other family and I arrived about the same time. All Chris said was, "Hey, Dad," as though I had just come in from work. I did not have much to say. I was angry and felt anything I said would make a bad situation worse, so I just kept my mouth shut. I signed some papers and thanked the people for caring for him. I told Chris to go get in the car. At this point, I just wanted to get him home and turn him over to the police. It was time for him to learn what a life of crime could do for him. We wanted him to go to trial and learn a lesson from what he had done and what he had put us through. However, I was glad we had found him and this nightmare had finally come to an end.

But the end was far from over. There was a long drive back to Alabama, and I was not interested in listening to the adventure. I just wanted justice. There was little said on the return trip. I did not feel like talking. I stopped in Chattanooga, Tennessee, and called the youth aid department and told them I had Chris and would be bringing him to them. But the youth aid detective told me, "Mr. Brady, we have no place for him. You will have to take him home, but you need to bring him in for a hearing next week." I just stood there with the phone to my ear, not believing what I was hearing. I hung up the phone and just stood there. I honestly did not want to take him home, not right now, but what choice did I have? Maybe if I had understood more about his mental state, I would have felt better, but right now I was tired and just wanted this all to come to an end. I had not slept for several days and could not think correctly. I did not want to get back in the car. All Chris wanted to know was where we were going to eat. I did not want to eat. I began to think I was losing it and maybe I needed to get some help. His mama was so glad to get him home and was willing to accept whatever came. Maybe all I wanted was vengeance.

My mother wrote a poem about a time when my brother had been gone for so many years, and she agonized and worried, not knowing where he was or if he was even alive. Even though Chris was gone for only eight days, it seemed much longer. My mother described it as the lonely years. When my brother returned home after such a long time gone, there was't any type of anger or questions of where he had been. Like the prodigal son, there was much rejoicing. I have to admit, I was angry, having seen what he had done, and I wanted him to pay. His mother had a different outlook, being relieved he was now home.

My mother wrote the following words when my brother was gone. They could also be Betsy's feelings when Chris was gone.

I wished upon a star that fell
And left a trail of light;
A wish to know just where you are
And what you are doing tonight.
I hear your voice in the whispering winds.

You sound so gay and free.
I see your face as the moon sails high,
And I'm sure you are smiling at me.
I see you now as in the long ago
Tramping the hills that you love best.

I feel your presence in the deepening gloom
When the elements are sweetly at rest.
I long so much to see you again,
But hope fades with each passing day.
I know not what tomorrow may bring.

Time has a habit of slipping away.
I have watched and waited for you
Until my eyes are dimmed by tears.
Do you know the heartache silence has caused

Throughout the lonely years?

I am praying a prayer for you, my son,
That wherever you may roam,
God will guide your footsteps right
And bring you safely home.

Life's Memories, Thelma Brady (page 42)

The hearing lasted all of fifteen minutes, with the judge sentencing him to fifteen hours of community service. I just stood there dumbfounded. I thought, You have got to be kidding me.

His community service consisted of crushing glass at a glass-recycling place. It was left up to us to get him there. I thought, Who is being punished here?

Many people with mental illness have almost no consideration or care for what they do, even when it is hurtful for those who love them the most. Chris would later say to his mother that that trip was the most fun he had ever had. He would not talk with me about the trip because he knew I did not want to hear it. Years later, we did discuss it, and I told him how I felt. There seemed to be no remorse for what he put us through. I was determined to have Chris serve some time for stealing my car and for what he had done. I felt strongly he needed to learn a lesson.

We soon discovered that Chris had little to no fear. He was not afraid of the police or anyone in authority. This would cause him many problems for the rest of his life. He only regretted doing something wrong when he got caught. He would later try to cover his tracks and become much more deceptive in what he was doing. He would stop short of doing anything criminal, or at least things people would press charges for. If they had pressed charges, he could have gone to jail. In our investigation, we found a person with bipolar disorder cares little about how the things he or she does affects those who love them the most. He would do things in front of us as though to say, "I'm going to do it, and you're not going to do anything about it." Betsy would call me at work and say, "I don't know what to do." Sometimes I would be on a cross-country trip flying with the United States Air Force Reserve. I had to work. I couldn't stay home all the time, and so much of the time the discipline fell into the hands of his mother. No kind of discipline worked, and we began to become even more frustrated having reached an end to our patience.

I do not believe that Chris, during this period of time, ever knew how much his mother would mean to him and how she would go to the extreme ends to try to save his life. It was unlike anything and beyond my comprehension as to why he did all of these things during these formative years. He later would exemplify the greatest love for his mother. He told people of how he loved his mother but felt he just had no control over his life. He told us, "The demons will not let me alone. They are in my head."

If we had only known what we were dealing with, perhaps we could have changed the course of his life. Doctors cannot treat an illness they know nothing about. Because of this, he would become almost unmanageable and had no fear. He was not afraid to fight if he needed to.

This lack of fear caused many problems not just with the police but also with experimenting with danger. He would do things like drive fast, even running from the police in his car and then later bragging about how he eluded them. How does this happen? Researchers have found children who are mentally ill have little fear of danger. They will do things such as lie down on the lanes in the middle of the highway, as though to say, "I dare you to hit me." Someone once said to me, "A person has to be out of their mind to do something like that. Surely they aren't thinking correctly when they play this kind of game." I have even said to Chris, "Are you out of your mind?" People say, "They must be strung out on drugs to do something like that." Often, that is the case.

With our children, there were many good times. They were not all bad. One might say there was always something interesting going on. There was joy, and there were tears. That's part of raising children. With some children, parents seem to experience no extreme difficulties. Others seem to always press the issue and want to have the last word.

As our children grew, there was always something to do at the Brady house. There was never a dull moment. When we began to raise teenagers, there were times when life was frustrating. All of this was normal part of parenting.

Children are born with different disorders that we as parents must learn to cope with. In teenage children, each one is different, and so it was with all five of our sons. Where one was extremely intelligent in books, another was well versed in the outdoors. One loved to fish; the other like to read and to draw. They were all different, each one having their own personality.

1 Timothy 5 talks about mothers teaching the younger women. So many things we learn from our parents. However, each mother and father must often rely upon natural instincts in knowing what is best for their children.

Someone once wrote humorously concerning the raising of children: "When a child turns thirteen, you put them in a box and feed them through a hole in the box. When they turn sixteen, you close up the hole." There may be some truth to that; of course, none of us are going to lock up our children and throw away the key, at least none who want the best for their children.

During this period of time, one has to change the form of discipline because spanking no longer works. Spanking only works when used consistently and without abuse, and this usually in small children. I am one who believed in spanking children but did not use that option very much. Discipline has to be administered differently.

In the course of ten years, Betsy and I were foster parents, having sixty-seven children. All were from many different backgrounds. Each one came with different problems, from abuse and neglect to experiencing things in their lives one would only read about. Every child had to be treated differently. Discipline had to be administered, but one had to be very careful that the punishment was compatible to the crime. We had discussed with our children about the needs in other children and how we all could minister to others. We decided to become foster parents but quit long before we started having problems with Chris.

Children of all ages respond to love, kindness, and patience. In the rearing of our children, we tried to make sure we used biblical standards. Each one of us will be held accountable to God for our children and the way we raised them. Children are a gift from God. He allows us to have them for a period of time, and he wants them back. It is up to parents to mold their children into godly people through example and teaching from God's Word.

The Psalmist wrote about children,

> Lo, children are an heritage of the Lord: and the fruit of the womb is his reward. As arrows are in the hand of a mighty man; so are children of the youth. Happy is the man that hath his quiver full of them.
>
> Psalm 127:3-5 (KJV)

They are a joy, and when they experience heartache, it begins to trouble the entire family unit. Where one is affected, all are in some way affected.

No one should take this responsibility lightly. Our life is our children. We delight when they excel and do good things. When they graduated from kindergarten, our children would say, "I am moving to the big school." We proudly watched our children as they walked across the stage to receive a diploma from high school and later from college.

Yes, as I have said, the raising of children during these tumultuous times takes patience, love, and kindness. We must exercise every biblical principle and listen to the advice of those who have gone before us. As time changes, we also have to change in the way we raise our children.

I was having a discussion with a minister who related to me a conversation with another minister who had reached retirement. He said he saw no difference in the raising of children in this age and time than he did when he was young. My minister friend asked him, "What planet did you come from?" He did not say that arrogantly, but the point was made—we are living in different times. He went on to say that when he was a boy growing up on the farm, he had never heard of marijuana or cocaine or many of the other things young people are experimenting with. Even the sexual experiments and experiences of young people today were not as open many years ago as they are now. Not to say they were not problems. There were, but we did not have so many distractions—such as iPods, television, movies, and so many other things that so much distracts us as parents—making it difficult to raise our children.

In our ever-changing world we must change the way we raise our families. Sometimes I think if we could go back in time to when life was simpler, perhaps we all would be better off. The one thing we should never change is the biblical way of raising children. God's Word will never be outdated.

Many books have been written about raising children, and much good advice comes from these books. We should always use the principles of the Bible not only in the relationships with others but in the relationships with our family. The Bible talks about kindness, compassion, love, and joy, often speaking about Jesus and the way he treated others. The Bible states in Ephesians 5:32 (KJV), "Be kind to each other, loving one another forgiving one another as God for Christ's sake hath forgiven you." The Bible does not tell us God will take away all the problems in our lives, but it does give us instruction on how to handle these problems when they come. Peter gave Christian virtues in 1 Peter 2, virtues that parents need in the rearing of children like patience and godliness.

Much prayer is needed, especially during these tumultuous times. My wife and I found ourselves praying often for each child. Chris had so many needs in his life and felt rejected by God, family, and others, which made it extremely difficult for us as parents to find the solutions that would ultimately save his life.

How does a parent find consolation that they have done the right thing? We felt, as parents standing beside the grave of our son, that we had not done enough during those most difficult times to steer him into a better direction before he hit the road that ultimately led to his death. It was an agonizing time for us as his parents to find the answers and find some form of normalcy in our life.

One of the most difficult times for us was to hear people say, "Watch out for that Brady boy. He's bad news. Don't let your children around him or go out with him. Lock your doors. Put your pocketbook up." I am not saying they were not justified in making those comments. Silently, we did the same thing. The next fourteen years would try our patience, our love, and our faith.

The years from thirteen to seventeen in Chris's life were very difficult. It was a time when we as parents questioned what we were going to do. You have already read just one story of a fourteen-year-old who ran away looking for other adventures, only to return home not having found what he was looking for. This left us exhausted, both mentally and emotionally. We even questioned how we could love and care for someone who at every corner, at every turn, would seem to be against everything we wanted to do, making it hard for us and the rest of the family.

There were four other sons who were also going through changes. We had to focus our attention on five different personalities. We had to make sure the situations we were facing with Chris did not destroy or affect our other children. To say it did not affect them would not be a true statement, for it did in many ways. At times, they were resentful and would question us, saying, "Why don't we just put Chris somewhere else? Why not send him to a boot camp to teach him a lesson?" He still had not been diagnosed with bipolar disorder but simply had some form of anger problems and might be mentally ill. He had been tested and retested, and at no time did those who were testing him diagnose or come to the conclusion that he had mental illness. No judge would send him away to a boot camp or confine him against his will, even though we were having these problems.

Over the next several years, Chris would have a number of girlfriends, with some older than him and even having their driver's license. He had the ability to attract beautiful girls. He had the charm, even to the point of convincing one mother we were going to beat him for being in her home. She took his side and told us we should not be so hard on him. If she had only known. But we did not tell her, neither were we unkind in what we said. We called the sheriff's department to have a talk with him because we did not know what else to do. We thought perhaps they might put some fear in him. We left his girlfriend's house, and as we turned on the main highway, we met the deputy sheriff's patrol car. I stopped then, telling them we had our son in the car. They had him get into the patrol car so they could talk with him. We did not hear the conversation, but he said they just tried to scare him. I asked him if he was scared. He replied, "Not much. They just talked mean to me like they could carry me to jail. I told them I hadn't done anything wrong." The deputies told me there were no warrants out on him, and we had not filed any charges and unless we went to the sheriff's department and did so they could not arrest him. To be honest, I don't know what I wanted them to do. It was late and we were tired, so we decided just to drop it and go home.

THEN CAME THE DRUGS

At first, there was marijuana. We found out later he sniffed gasoline because it gave him a sense of being high. There was nonstick spray that, when sprayed up the nostrils, produces a high. He only tried this, he said, one time but did not like it because it gave him headaches.

According to Teen Drug-Abuse Facts at eHow.com http://www.ehow.com,

> In addition to abusing alcohol and tobacco products—such as cigarettes or chewing tobacco—teenagers also abuse a number of other drugs. According to an article by Dr. Roxanne Dryden-Edwards—a psychiatrist who works with adults, children, and adolescents—the following drugs are commonly abused by teenagers:

- Marijuana
- Cold medications, such as Sudafed and Benadryl
- Depressants and stimulants, which alter the emotional state

- Dangerously addicting narcotics, many of which are meant to be used as painkillers. These include morphine, codeine and Vicodin

- Drugs like Ecstasy, known as "club drugs"

- Teens also breathe in the vapors of harmful aerosols, such as gasoline or paint.

Most parents, at first, deny their child is taking drugs. We were religious people and thought, This does not happen to us. We lived in a small rural community. We were dumb when it came to drugs and their use. We had never seen any except at the county fair, where the police had them on display. One day, we found something growing in a pot and discovered it was a marijuana plant.

Things began to get more difficult. So it is with so many families who struggle with children experimenting with drugs. Don't get me wrong; we never stopped loving our son. We hated what he was doing to us, to himself, to his brothers, and to others around him. We never stopped looking for ways to help him, to understand him, and to deal with his problems. I grew up in Pintlala, Alabama, a small rural community fifteen miles south of Montgomery, Alabama, on US Highway 31. One would've never thought this small community would ever have to deal with drugs. A neighbor who had grown up there commented to me, "I cannot believe we have a drug problem this close to where we live." My reply to him was, "Drugs are within rock-throwing distance from here." The most common drugs for our community were crack cocaine and marijuana. Experimenting with marijuana led to the day when Chris smoked his first rock. Drugs affect every community, large or small. This blight on our society has destroyed the homes of good people all over the world. Yes, wherever your community is—whether in the great state of California or the

Sunshine State of Florida or Hometown, Alabama—drugs are a problem. They are not going to go away.

Many of us can look back over the turbulent times of the sixties and remember the hippie movement. We have seen them on television and read about them in the paper. No one during that period of time would have ever dreamed we would be at the point we are now. Who knows where we'll be if we don't get some type of handle on the drug problem. Don't think drugs are for the big cities or the ghettos. Understand they are in small-town USA, even across the street.

On our property, there is a small pond with a small boathouse we rarely went into. One day, I decided to go and check out the pond and found drug paraphernalia. In this case, there was a Coke can that was mashed in the middle with burn marks on it. There was some rubbing alcohol, a razor blade, and some other items—I did not know what they were. I knew Chris was on the hard stuff. I didn't know what crack cocaine was at that time, nor did I know what it would do to an individual.

Talking to him several years later, I said, "If you want to quit, you could quit." His reply to me was, "Daddy, you just don't understand." Those were some powerful words that would be repeated over and over. I did not know. My biggest problem was (and for other parents it might be too) I couldn't comprehend the power drugs have on people.

Many years ago, people would freebase cocaine. This is where they would cook it using particular solvents, but this was physically dangerous, and often there would be an explosion ignited by the fire, which left people burned and severely injured. People began to experiment and came up with what is commonly known as "crack." I personally have never seen any crack, only the results of a long binge.

One day, I decided I would sit down with Chris and have him explain to me exactly how the drug made him feel. He would always tell me that there was just no explaining it. He said to me, "Daddy, words have not been made to explain what happens when I smoke this rock. After I smoke it, sometimes I want to die because I am unable to deal with the results of not having this feeling. This feeling only lasts for a very short few minutes, and sometimes it fades as fast as it came, and then I need another rock."

I was trying to come up with an explanation for people to understand what we had to deal with for eleven years and what other parents were dealing with. People at church, preachers, and well-meaning family members all had advice for something they knew nothing about. They did not know what the parents and the family of a "crack head" lived with every day.

Yes, well-meaning people gave advice, but in Chris's words: "You don't have a clue. Don't you know I want to quit? I get paid on Friday, and on Saturday night, I have no money left. I hate what it does to my family, but when I'm taking the drug, I don't care about my family, about whether they have food or even a place to live. I just want more crack. If I can't get it with the money I have, I will steal what you have in order to get it." Those were Chris's very words in our conversation, and I saw something I had been missing. Chris hated what he was doing to us. He was a good person, gentle at times, and extremely sad about what he was doing, but he had no control.

In this discussion, one would have thought I was talking to a college professor. The conversation was intelligent and thought provoking. Don't think all crackheads are stupid people. They are only stupid because they got involved with drugs. I didn't know what to say. After this, we began to talk more, but it did little to curb his drug usage.

Crack is one of the worst drugs on the market today. In conversation with a policeman from Long Beach, Mississippi, he said of all drug dealers, he hates the crack dealers the most. Drug dealers pushing drugs on the youth of our country should be executed if they're found guilty. They are responsible for killing the youth of our land and have no remorse. But putting all drug users in jail is not the answer, nor will it work. People say of the user, "Put them in jail," and I would say, "They don't care if you put them in jail." All a crack head wants is another rock, and they don't care how they get it.

On the west side of Montgomery, Alabama, one can travel down Mobile Road and see prostitutes hanging out or just walking up and down the street in hopes that someone will stop and pick them up. This is the same scene all over the United States. I traveled this way to work every day to Maxwell Air Force Base. Young women would be walking along the street, having just left one of the cheap hotels on that side of town. They are all where they are because of drugs. They don't care what anyone thinks or what it does to their families. Some have children at home, but for now, they must get some money to support their habit. The police have sting operations to round them up, but as soon as they are released, they are back again. The cycle continues.

Why, you might ask, does a person continue to use the drug? Perhaps the following chapter can give you some idea of why.

PLEASURE UNSPEAKABLE

According to www.cocaine.org:

To obtain crack-cocaine, ordinary cocaine is concentrated by heating the drug in a solution of baking soda until the water evaporates. This type of base-cocaine makes a cracking sound when heated, hence the name "crack." Base-cocaine vaporizes at a low temperature, so it can be easily inhaled via a heated pipe or some use a soda can mashed down in the middle. A small hole is put in the middle and the smoker inhales through the end of the can.

Crack-cocaine delivers an intensity of pleasure completely outside the normal range of human experience. It offers the most wonderful state of consciousness, and the most intense sense of being alive, the user will ever enjoy. The user will access heightened states of being unknown to normal people. Looking for adequate words, crack-takers sometimes speak of the rush in terms of a "whole-body orgasm."

www.cocaine.org

"I really don't know how to explain it. My whole body seems like it's going to explode with pleasure. It feels so good, and I don't want it to end," said Chris. The problem is it does end and quickly. Some have reported staying high for three to four minutes, but Chris said sometimes the feeling left almost as fast as it came, and he said, "I light another rock as quick as I can, and sometimes that feeling would not be anything like the one I just had. I smoke more, hoping I could get the same feeling I had earlier." How can something that leads a person to the edge of heaven take them to the verge of hell? Chris had often referred to hell after taking the drug. He said, "Daddy, it's like having sex. The pleasure of smoking crack will last only a short time, sometimes three to five minutes, but most of the time, shorter. Sometimes I will have more rocks next to me, and I will have another orgasm and another and another until all my rocks are gone, and then I start falling, as though on some cliff somewhere, but there is no rope to catch my fall, and I scream. It seems bugs are crawling all over me, coming out my ears, nose, and mouth. I sometimes vomit."

He said sometimes he cried after the high left him if he was out of money. He curled up into a ball and fell into a deep sleep. He said sometimes he passed out from exhaustion only to find himself in a ditch where the drug dealers had dropped him after all his money was gone.

Some drug dealers are good to the user, expecting them to return when they have more money, even treating them as though they were good friends. The truth is drug dealers care nothing for the user. They are treated like garbage. Many drug dealers do not usually use drugs themselves and prey on those who do. At times, I heard Chris refer to those who were supplying the drugs as his friends. He would even become angry with me when I would say to him, "Son, they are not your friends. Believe me. They are not your friends."

Drug dealers are worse than animals. They'll discard the user like a bad piece of meat when their money runs out. Chris never would say this happened to him, but listening to other users, some drug dealers will start pimping them, giving them just enough drugs to keep them in submission. This happens more in young girls and women than men; however, some men have been sodomized during the height of their drug usage.

I began to do more research to try to understand the drug. You cannot help someone if you do not know what they are dealing with. I went to the Internet and found a Web site (biopsychiatry.com/cocainedep.html) that had a lot of information. In short, they said,

> As a rule of thumb, it is profoundly unwise to take crack-cocaine. Do not even experiment with it because it will hook you the first time one uses the drug.
>
> The brain has evolved a truly vicious set of negative feedback mechanisms. Their functional effect is to stop us from being truly happy for long. Nature is cruelly parsimonious with pleasure. The initial pleasure is short-lived and is uniquely powerful and is followed by a "crash."
>
> What happens next is anxiety, depression, irritability, extreme fatigue and possibly paranoia. Physical health often will deteriorate. An intense craving for more cocaine develops. Severe depressive conditions may follow; agitated delirium; and also a syndrome sometimes known as toxic paranoid psychosis. The neural after-effects of chronic cocaine use include changes in the brain which takes a person into pleasurable experiences however there is the down-regulation to compensate for their drug-induced over stimulation.

I refer to the "happy side of the brain," which is now damaged forever. Even if a person quits the drug, this never heals. Thus, the brain's capacity to experience pleasure is diminished.

From the first time an individual uses the drug, he or she can never be totally happy again without the stimulation of crack. In my discussions with Chris and others who are addicted or have been addicted to this drug, they always felt extremely saddened after coming off a binge. What I have found in my investigation, and in what I have seen in my own son, is a drug that totally destroys a personality. It leaves an individual without a conscience and caring only for him or herself, seeking to be happy when there's no way but the drug. Hence, as you will read, the drug is called, among many other things, "the selfish drug."

The article also said,

> The social consequences of heavy use can be equally unpleasant. Non-recreational users are likely eventually to alienate family and friends. They tend to become isolated and suspicious. Most of their money and time is spent thinking about how to get more of the drug. The compulsion may become utterly obsessive. The illusion of free-will is likely to disappear. During a "mission," essentially a 3–4 day crack-binge, users may consume up to 50 rocks a day.

Chris was never gone for very long periods of time, which made me wonder if the drug loses its power or the user becomes too exhausted to continue. As with alcohol or any other drug, a person's body will start shutting down, and a person will die. Not from the drug, but because the body itself has not received any nourishment and becomes dehydrated.

After a payday, Chris would often disappear and only reappear when all his money was gone. To obtain more, he would lie, cheat, and steal. We know of some who would commit crimes of violence, but to my knowledge, Chris never hurt anyone but himself.

Chris, at one point, told me when he was at the very height of drug usage or a binge, he did not care if he lived or died. When he was taking the drug, nothing mattered. He told me all he could think about was how to get another rock. He, as well as others, told me money is often what triggers the desire for the drug. Never give money to a person you suspect is taking drugs. Also remember that crack is cheaper than most drugs. One can get a rock for a few dollars.

Experts believe crack is the most addictive drug on the market today. In the 2009 National Drug Threat Assessment released by the National Drug Intelligence Center, cocaine is identified as the leading drug threat to society. Cheaper than cocaine in powdered form that's either sniffed or mixed with water and injected, crack use has spread like wildfire across all demographics. From Hollywood stars, to Wall Street businessmen, to housewives, to experimenting teens, to back-alley bums, crack knows no boundaries. It doesn't look to be stopping anytime soon, despite projected short-term shortages.

What is the answer, and where are we as a nation headed? There is no stopping the sale of drugs to our children until we as a nation get angry and say to our leaders, "Enough." We should be fighting to save our children from diseases we do not understand. Many books and articles have been written on mental illness and on drug usage. There is a lot of instruction. We must get this information into the hands of those who need it the most. Parents are agonizing every day over children they cannot help and over situations they have no control. Support groups dealing with these situations can talk about and encourage and support one another. These things are well and good, but we as parents need to have the support of those in the political realm to introduce legislation that will help us.

I'm angry with myself for not knowing more about drugs and mental illness and not understanding my son and the agony that he was going through. I did not comprehend when he said to me, "The demons will not leave me alone." I had the attitude that he was the one that needed to straighten up and get his life right.

The question is, where is the grant to get rid of the drug dealers, the very people who are destroying the youth of our nation? Why give such a small amount of money to law enforcement to fight a growing drug problem? Where is the money for more programs to teach our youth of the dangers of drugs, premarital sex, and so many things that damage their lives? Must we lose the entire generation before we as a nation wake up? Our sheriff told me, "I don't have the resources to close down all the crack houses. I know where they are, but we do not have the money or the manpower to police all these places."

Millions of people all over the United States and the world wake up every day and fight a disease they know so little about. Yes, we have learned the symptoms of bipolar disorder. There is treatment, but again, it is an expensive treatment. There is no reason for people who have a mental illness not to live a normal life, for there are medications that will help. I do not have the answers, only having wrestled with this problem in my family, but I know where it will lead if it is untreated. It destroys the health of the parents, leaving us exhausted and, many times, financially ruined. It is imperative we recognize in the early age that there is a problem.

How many times have I wished I could go back again for a second chance. There are no more chances. God only gives us one opportunity to live upon this earth. If there are things going on within your family among your children and you do not understand why, please get some advice. It may be nothing, but then again, it may be a lot. Bipolar disorder and drugs do not mix; it will only lead to an explosion.

What you are reading is not fiction but truth, and we had no answers, only tears. We were frustrated beyond words as to what to do and where to go. We basically were financially ruined, and with no more money to help Chris fight his battle, it seemed the drug dealers would be the winners.

I cannot tell you how many times we watched our son be led away in handcuffs, being guilty of a crack addiction and mental illness. I watched the police put him in the backseat of the car and take him away. On one occasion, when the police came to his house to arrest Chris, I asked them, "Please do not put the handcuffs on him in front of his mother." However, one day, while in court after being sentenced, as we sat there, a deputy came up behind him and put on the handcuffs with his mother looking on. This was almost more than I could endure, for I saw the look in her eyes as they led him away. He took one more look at us as the deputy ushered him out of the courtroom. We just sat there with a knot in our stomachs.

Consumed

Chris obtained work with a yard service. He loved to work outside and was good at landscaping and making a yard look beautiful. He took the test to become a certified landscaper and eventually had a number of very good jobs, even supervising a large company out of Atlanta, Georgia, with a good salary. Chris had a way of taking a yard and turning a ditch into a beautiful landscape. Three days before his death, I watched him prune some trees. When completed, he said, "Look at that artwork, pop! Ain't that beautiful?" I had to admit, "Son, that does look good." Yes, he had a talent that was being wasted.

At one point, Chris had somehow been able to get his addiction under control. One day, he came home and informed us he was going to join the Army National Guard. We thought it was a good thing, for it would teach him some discipline that I was unable to give him and he was unwilling to accept. He went off to basic training, and although over the next several months he would complete the training, there were many difficulties he had to overcome. The biggest was authority. He constantly had problems with the drill instructors. They cut him no slack, and life for him, as a recruit, was hard. He could not walk away, which was good. He could not, without great consequences, talk back to the instructor. The military was a different way of life than he had ever experienced. Finally, the day came when he was to graduate from basic training. We traveled to Augusta, Georgia, to attend the graduation ceremonies. We were proud of him as we saw him march down the field.

Yes, it was a happy time, and we all celebrated. After spending some time with him, we returned home to Alabama, and Chris traveled on to Virginia to begin more training for a career he would have in the army. After completion of school, he returned home to Alabama, but it was not the same. At a welcome home party in our home, his friends came, and among those was his girlfriend. She later told me Chris was not the same person; that he was different than what she had known before. It was as if he were switching personalities.

He had personality switches, which could be seen in his eyes as though saying, "Let me alone." He dated this young lady a few times, but she was fast to learn he was not the person she wanted as a husband. She was very spiritual-minded and could not handle the smoking and continual personality changes.

One of the things we learned about bipolar disorder was the inability to accept failure and to accept broken relationships. It causes a person to believe they cannot succeed in anything, leaving a feeling of rejection. Chris, over the next several months, spasmodically attended his monthly National Guard meetings, which led to him being discharged from the National Guard for non-participation.

He also entered several relationships, but they would not last. His drug use was increasing. He had no money to pay for the drugs. He turned to the only place where money could be obtained: stealing from us. If there were any big mistakes made early on, it was here. We thought what we were doing was right in our own hearts. We could not stand the thought of our son being out on the street at night with nothing to eat and nowhere to go. I lacked the courage to have him locked up.

There was not much left to steal, and so he turned to our friends, other relatives, and neighbors. As the drugs consumed Chris, we were consumed to try to find the answer. How do we make him quit? There is no making a crackhead quit. They must hit the bottom as I have said before. There is no making them quit just because you as a parent or loved one has had enough. As time went on, even though I loved Chris, there seemed to be a separation between him and me. No longer could I tolerate the things he did.

In all of this, his mother never turned her back on him. I made many statements over the years that I regret. I wish they could be taken back. No one can take back something said. Statements like that cause much grief. I believed myself to be justified in the way I felt, the things I said, and even the things I did. There was nothing I could say or do to change the way he was treating us as a family. This led to resentment of his brothers. Later, after his death, they could only say, "I wish we had done more." They felt they had let him down. This was not the case, but we were all filled with guilt. Trying to reassure them, I told them what happened to Chris was not their fault. We had done all we could, but in the end, we lost.

Chris continued to go into deep depression and come out again. Each time, it seemed he looked a little different, a little more haggard. He was a little more distant than the time before. We did not know where to turn. One day, I found where Chris had been using drugs, and I turned to the sheriff's department for help. My brother and I went to the sheriff's department and had a meeting with the Montgomery County Sheriff. He was sympathetic and explained we were not the only ones with this problem. I told him I did not know what else to do and where else to go. He took me down the hall to talk to a drug enforcement officer. They could only advise me as to what to do. It did little to curtail his drug usage. They could not come and lock him up, for there were no warrants out on him.

One day, we came home from work, only to notice he had taken all of the items we had purchased for Christmas and returned them for the money. That year, we purchased Christmas three times. Our television, VCR, and so many other items were stolen. I went around to the local pawnshops to find these items. Sometimes I would buy them back if the price was not too high. Why did we not press charges? We kept saying that we did not want him in jail. In my frustration, I commented to a local pawnshop owner of how he knew the items they were taking in were stolen. He replied, "If you parents would do a better job raising your children, then you would not be having this problem." I am sure all pawnshop owners do not feel that way. My conversation with this man would do little to ease my frustrations and my anger. The pawnshop owner said that all a pawnshop was required to do was turn in a list to the sheriff's department once a month of all items taken in. Some of the items I recovered, some I did not, until one day, I said, "Enough."

One day, some of my tools were missing, and I knew who had taken them and where they were. I had gone to the pawnshops until I found them. I reported this to the Montgomery County Sheriff's Department and filed charges against Chris. I struggled with my feelings and wept about over what I had done. I could not sleep that night because I had heard all the horror stories of people being assaulted in their jail cells. I was being tormented for doing the right thing. Chris was an adult and had to take on the adult responsibility for what he had done. The sheriff told me that as long as Chris was in jail, he could not get drugs. This did little to make me feel better. I could hear his mother crying at night and worrying about Chris. Sometimes I would wake up, and she would not be in the bed. I'd get up to check on her, only to find her drinking a cup of coffee in the corner of our back porch. From that vantage point, one could see our driveway, and she often sat there and waited for him or one of our other sons to come home. Betsy never gave up on Chris. When everyone else had given up, she had not. On this night, we were both broken up and did not know what to do next. Where would it end? When would we get the phone call? Where was he? Was he lying in some crack house in a drunken stupor and wallowing in filth until the crack house owner had all his money and kicked him out on the street? Yes, these were our thoughts on so many occasions. These are the thoughts of so many good parents who must deal with just such a situation.

I told myself, "He is an adult and has to take on responsibility for his actions. He cannot continue this way. We cannot go on this way. Things have to get better, and we are doing what is best for him at this time." I went through all of these thoughts in my mind and in conversations with Betsy. We sat on the corner of our porch and discussed what was happening. We did not know what to do. We prayed God would lead us in the right decisions. We asked God to lead us, to help us find some peace in what we were doing.

Saturday came around, and it was time to go to visit Chris in jail. We were nervous. This was our first time, and we did not know what to expect. We thought we would go there to the jail and they would bring him out into a room. Sitting there, we could all talk. There would be hugging and giving encouragement. It was far from what we had expected. We had rehearsed what we would say to him, even to the point of saying we were sorry we had him arrested. I should say I had him arrested, for his mother had nothing to do with it. This is one area I tried to protect her because I knew what it was doing to her on the inside.

We learned we were not the only family going through this crisis. Like mental illness, crack cocaine has no boundaries. It affects good people, good families, and church going people––rich and poor. It affects the educated and the uneducated. We were not alone, but this did little to make us feel better.

While waiting to visit Chris, we met another couple that lived north of Montgomery who was also visiting their son. They were good people from a fine, Christian family. They were a family who went to church every Sunday and did all the right things, and like us, they were questioning where they went wrong. This is a question all good parents ask when their children do the things they should not do.

The father was like me, to some degree. He took a harder line on his son than his wife. However, I would visit Chris, and he would not. His son did not want his father there to see him. Chris and I never did break ties with one other. This father did not have the closeness with his son. It was only the mother who would go back and visit.

It is not easy to go to jail and visit a child. We had heard the horror stories about people getting raped and all types of molestation and the beatings and the fights that go on in jail. I am sure much has been over exaggerated, but still, it does happen, and we were very worried about Chris. He told us he had no place to sleep, and we knew it was true. The jail was very overcrowded. He really made it sound much worse than it was, or so we thought. He was hoping to convince us to bail him out. We would later put our house up as collateral to get him out, but not this time.

We had a conversation with the deputy in charge. We got there early so we might be able to see Chris and spend more time with him. We found out we could only see him for a few minutes. In our conversation with the deputy, we expressed our extreme concern for our son and what might happen to him inside the jail. She tried to ease our concern and said, "I assure you, Mr. and Mrs. Brady, your son will be fine. He gets three meals a day, and if he needs a doctor, he will have one. If he desires spiritual counseling, he can have that. He just cannot walk out that door." A jail is meant to be a dark, dreary place. A place where one will not want to go back. It is a place to be feared, a place to stay away from. I found the jails I visited to be that and more.

Our time came, our names were called, and we looked at one another. I grabbed Betsy's hand. We stood up, hesitating almost, afraid to go through those doors. We went back to talk to Chris. It was not what we had expected. We were assigned a booth and could only talk on a telephone and look at him through the glass. This broke my heart, and it was all I could do to sit there and listen to him beg. He knew it was my decision—and mine alone——that kept him in jail.

I kept telling myself that he was in a place where he could not hurt himself nor get drugs. Yet we cried and we asked, "Why?" Most people will never have to experience the effect this has upon their lives. To sit there and look at a child through glass and not be able to touch him has a devastating effect. Gone were all of the things Chris had done. All of these things were all gone because sitting there on the other side of that glass was our child, and in this moment, we could not touch him. I asked him how he was doing and tried to make small talk, but I knew what he wanted. He began to beg, "Mama and Daddy please get me out of here. I want to come home. You just don't know what it's like in here." We wanted to, and we even talked about if we should.

We decided the best thing to do was leave him in jail, which was one of the hardest decisions we had ever made. We felt it was for his own good and also for our own peace of mind. He needed to learn he could not continue breaking the law and have other people always bail him out of every bad situation. We sat there as parents, and as we listened, we debated on whether we should take him home with us that day. These are decisions parents have to make in bad situations, and sometimes, we allow our emotions to overcome us. We allow all of the love we have for our children to be used, sometimes not in the best way. We do not want to practice "tough love." We only see what is before us at that particular time. Our child begged and cried, wanting to come home, and we had the power to make it happen.

The meeting finally was over. We hung up the telephone, and he looked at us. He knew how to get to us. His lips formed the words, "I love you." Chris had a way to make us change our minds. It is hard to practice tough love. On this day, he almost succeeded again. He stood up, having already been briefed by the guards, "When we tell you your time is up, you are to get up right then and return to your cell." He looked tired, withdrawn, and extraordinarily sad. We stood there and watched him go through the steel doors in his prison garments. It didn't look like Chris. Our son in striped baggy pants and shirt—jail garments. The last thing he said before hanging up the phone was, "I cannot believe you are going to leave me here over Christmas," and my reply was, "Believe it." I don't know if I believed it, but nevertheless, I was at least, for now, determined.

After Chris got out of jail, it did not end there. Either he was going to win or I was going to teach him a lesson. At what cost would this lesson be? I thought he had learned his lesson and did not want to go back to jail. I believe he really tried for a time, but he was consumed.

Chris stole a new chainsaw I had purchased and sold it for a few dollars to obtain drugs. The saw was still in the box. When I arrived home and found it gone, I was very upset. I knew immediately what had become of it. There were two things I decided at this very moment. First, Chris was not going to get away with this one. Second, the pawnshop that had purchased it was going to lose money. The first thing I did was visit the local pawnshops. They all knew Chris, as they know all those who frequent their shops on a regular basis. It did not take me long. I located the chainsaw and, having all of this information, went to the sheriff's department and swore out a warrant for Chris. I then went before a judge to ask for a high bail, even though this was a minor offense. She did assign the bail at $3,000, the maximum she could give for this crime. I was angry and hoping he would have to stay in jail a little while longer.

The sheriff's department told me they would not go looking for him so they could arrest him. I cried out, "What do you mean you are not going to look for him? All you have to do is go to my house and arrest him." They would not investigate this crime because it was a misdemeanor. I was informed if they stopped him on a traffic violation, they could arrest him for it. I literally thought I was going to pop. You have got to be kidding me, I thought. All I have been through and you are not even going to go get him? At this point, I thought I was losing it. The sheriff's department did send out a deputy to the pawnshop to retrieve the chainsaw, which was to be used as evidence if he ever came to trial. This was the second thing I meant to happen. The pawnshop lost their money. At least something good came from it.

Chris was to have a court appearance in a few days following this on another minor traffic offense. Believe me, at this point, I was out for vengeance. I do not believe I wanted justice. I hadn't even started the saw up. He was going to learn a lesson. If all this was true, why did I feel so guilty about what I was doing? I am deceiving him, I thought.

I arranged with a deputy to have him arrested when he entered the courthouse. They said they could do this. Driving him to the courthouse, I almost turned around as we talked about different things. We made small talk. I had calmed down. Time has a way of doing this. My heart was heavy to know what I was about to do over something that did not cost us very much money. I kept telling myself this was the right thing to do, for he needed to learn he could not steal people's property, whether it was from his mom or dad, uncle or aunt, or close friend. He had to understand there was a penalty—a price to pay—for these crimes. I dropped Chris off in front of the courthouse and told him I would be waiting down the street. When I pulled over, I called the deputy and told him, "Chris is on his way into the courthouse." In a few minutes, he called me and said, "We have your son in custody."

I cried because of this deception. I felt I had put him in jail only to prove a point. I knew this was not true. It did little to make me feel any better having done it. I just sat there one block south of the county courthouse, depressed, knowing Chris was, at that moment, being fingerprinted.

I began to reason that it wasn't my fault. He did this to himself. I had to do it, but with all the thoughts and the questions, I just could not get over my deception. That's the way I saw it. It was not me who had put him there. Was it not the low-life drug dealers who were the recipients of the few dollars he got for my chainsaw?

It was a difficult time for me over the next several days to try to deal with what I had done. Later, when I saw Chris, he said to me, "Daddy, if you had only told me." I said, "Son, you would not have gone if I told you." He was there because of his crime. He was not able to make bail, and no one would sign the bail for him.

Several days later, he got out; he never did tell me how or who bailed him out. When he went before the judge, I stood beside him. She fined him, gave him probation, and gave him several months to pay the fine. All of this for a saw that cost $120. But it made no difference, for the cycle continued.

It does not matter what our children may do, they are still our children. We try to protect them, if we can. In conversations with other people who experienced some of the things we had, we learned the feelings we were having were normal. It was normal to feel the frustration, anger, and, oftentimes, the loneliness that comes with having a child who is mentally ill with a drug addiction.

After Chris's death, my brother, Allen, talked with the sheriff of our county and thanked him for all he had done for his nephew, and his reply was, "If I just kept him in jail, this might not have happened." Allen assured him he had done all he legally could have done. Nobody was responsible for this terrible tragedy, perhaps not even Chris. We all wanted to blame one another, the law, and the people he ran around with. The list went on and on as to who would be to blame. The cycle continued.

MARRIAGE, DRUGS, AND MENTAL ILLNESS

In 1997 Chris began dating a young lady from Montgomery he had attended school with. Over the period of time that Chris was dating her, things seemed to be going well. He did not seem to be taking drugs but was wrestling with bouts of depression. He had a job working with a local landscaper, where he was doing well. The day came when he decided he wanted to get married. Working with his fiancée's parents, it was decided the wedding would be at our home in Pintlala. We had built a rustic house on our home place, nestled back in the edge of the woods surrounded by big oak trees. Other weddings were conducted here because of the beautiful setting, and so it was with Chris's wedding.

Betsy had been a caterer, owning a catering company in Montgomery, and knew how to put on a wedding. She was proud of Chris and wanted this to be special. We were happy parents. Tuxedos were picked up for him and all his brothers and for me. I performed the wedding, as I had done for our two older sons. It turned to be a beautiful wedding, and we were so happy for Chris, for it seemed his life had changed. We were going to enjoy the moment, and we did. Many people came to the wedding, for we have a big family and a great church family who stood beside us in the dismal times. Betsy did her best on this wedding, as though it cost a million dollars. We thought that perhaps if he had a beautiful, special wedding, it would show him how much people cared for him and wanted to see him succeed in life. We had often said it would seem to us the more we tried, the harder it became.

The wedding was beautiful. Chris was handsome, and his bride was beautiful. What more could one ask? Life was good. We were so happy because we saw him smiling and thought that this was a new beginning for him.

His mother put on the best. Out under the trees in our backyard with spotlights shining upon the cakes, it was such a beautiful setting. Nothing could be better. The wedding was a success. The sky was beautiful. There was not a cloud in the sky. However, we did not see the cloud approaching that could destroy such a beautiful event, a cloud that would turn into a storm. For now, the sky was clear. It seemed this could be a great marriage. People came by and congratulated Chris and hugged him and his new bride. His friends had decorated the car as they were about to take off on the honeymoon and a new life.

One of the big problems Chris had was his ability to attract police, and on the honeymoon was no exception. Chris got a speeding ticket on the honeymoon night. We all thought it was funny that he was in a hurry to get to the honeymoon part.

Things were going well, and we were all happy. Chris was not using drugs anymore, or so we thought. Drug addicts are the world's best in covering their tracks. This we didn't know, for we thought he was clean. Now he had a reason to clean up his life.

He moved his new wife to Mobile, where he started a land-scaping business. After a period of time in Mobile, he met some people that introduced him to drug dealers. There is no place one can go to escape the dealers. No place one can hide, for drugs of any kind, of any flavor, can be found. Changing locations will increase the chances of being able to break the habit, but not always, because the individual is still a drug addict.

Chris's crack addiction began to take a toll on his new wife. They were doing well with her working at a local bank and him making good money. As with all drug addicts, most of the money went for drugs. Drugs mixed with mental illness are bad partners in a marriage. Many marriages do not survive it, and Chris's was no exception. The pressures are often more than a wife or a husband can bear. It creates all types of problems and leaves most families bankrupt.

Chris and his wife could not remain in Mobile and, because of the seriousness of the crack situation, returned to Montgomery. The toll on his marriage was serious and caused them to separate for a while.

Even under very good circumstances, people have problems making marriages work. Couples must always be willing to face situations that come their way. As a minister, I have helped young people deal with many situations in their marriages—everything from sexual to financial issues. I found myself unable to find the answer to help my own son. I was always able to help others but felt I was unable to come to the rescue within my own family. My wife has often said, "Save the world, and lose your family." It was true; it is true—we as ministers sometimes fail to realize the difficulties our families face just because their husband or father happens to be the local minister.

What would I do, and where would I go to find the answers? I solicited the advice of those close to me and usually always got the same answer. So often they would say, "The Bible says this," or "The Bible says that." I knew all of that, and I trusted in God and still do today. I just had no answer for how to break the cycle. I would get angry and say things I would later regret, but the frustrations of dealing with it all sometimes would be hard to overcome. At times, I just wanted him out, but his mother was another story. She never cast him aside. It was as though she felt she was going the help him win the battle. I do not believe she ever felt she would lose the battle, for if one prays enough and continues with a strong faith, there is no battle that cannot be won. She truly believed this, as you will read, over and over. Faith can move mountains.

Jesus taught us about faith in Matthew 17:21 (KJV), "If ye have faith as a grain of mustard seed, ye shall say unto this mountain, Remove hence to yonder place; and it shall remove; and nothing shall be impossible unto you."

Betsy's faith never wavered. It was beyond her motherly instincts to help him. Drug usage began to get worse, as Chris spent all his money on drugs. He was constantly looking for drugs. As a result, he lost his job, and things began to get worse. Chris had still not been diagnosed with bipolar disorder, and yet, the signs were all there: low self-esteem, dependency upon drugs, and the neglect of his family. I thought him to be just another crack head. To sit back and watch a family member disintegrate before our eyes was difficult and heart wrenching.

One day, after Chris and his wife had returned from Mobile, he was living with us for a period of time while he and his wife were trying to work out their problems. Chris had not come home, and no one had seen him.

In the afternoon, with Betsy in the house, Chris stumbled out of the forest located behind our house. Insects had bitten him all over and gotten into his hair and clothing. He was very sick. His mother asked him what was wrong. He told her he had taken a lot of pills of different kinds. Betsy rushed him to the hospital, where the doctors pumped his stomach. They then began to try to find out why he took the medicine. This would be his first attempt to commit suicide. We begged him to get help, but he said all was okay and that we were making a big deal out of nothing.

Chris attempted suicide another time behind his house in Montgomery. Betsy, his wife and one of her friends happened to be in the house visiting. They walked around behind the house just in time to see Chris step off a chair with a rope around his neck.

What kind of problems did Chris have to cause him to do this? We could only guess. He had been out the night before in one of the local crack houses, smoking. Up to this moment, we thought everything was fine. He and his wife were back together, rented a house, and appeared to be happy. Chris also had returned to work. Betsy did not know why she went around behind the house instead of going in the front door. For some reason, she decided to walk around the house. She saw him step off the chair with a rope around his neck. She frantically ran to him, grabbed him, and screamed for his wife to call 911. Chris was a big man, weighing over two hundred pounds. As he was hanging there choking, Betsy pushed up while his wife's friend took the rope from around his neck. When things like this happen, it seems everything automatically goes into slow motion. You are just reacting and doing what you know needs to be done at that time.

Mothers usually react according to instinct and without thinking. We have read of mothers who have given their lives for their children in a frantic effort to save them. Betsy was doing all she could as a mother to save his life.

There are people who say they have the answers to all these situations. Many say there is absolutely no reason a person should take their life, especially when there are those who love them.

A deputy with the Montgomery County Sheriff's Department, who had befriended Chris, was called to come over to help convince him that he needed to go to the hospital. He finally persuaded him to go to Jackson's hospital to be evaluated. The deputy even took him there and stayed with him until he was admitted. While in the Jackson Hospital psychiatric unit, many tests were conducted on Chris to determine the nature of his illness.

While all this was going on, I made the decision to have Chris committed to the psychiatric hospital in Montgomery. This was one of the hardest decisions I have ever made but felt it necessary to save his life. I cried, for it is a difficult thing for one to finally admit your son is out of control. What were we to do? Where were we to go? To go to a drug rehab was very expensive, and Chris had no insurance. We had spent all the money we had and were in debt almost beyond our ability to repay.

SEARCHING FOR HELP

I sat in my car outside of the hospital and cried like a baby. Two suicide attempts and only God knows what else he had done to himself. Someone had to do something. We cannot continue living this way, I thought. Chris needed help. As I sat there in my car, my mind went back to when he was a child and all the good times we had shared together.

This beautiful child, now a man, was in big trouble. As a father, I'm supposed to know what to do, but that day, I could only sit there and cry. Again, I asked the question, "Why me, God? Why me? I have been your faithful servant. I have tried to live a godly life and be a good father and husband and provider. I do not understand the test of my faith today. Show me the way, and guide my footsteps."

I was so tired and had been up for so many hours without sleep, and it was taking its toll on me. As I sat there in my car, I dozed off. I was not asleep long, but during that time, I saw Chris hanging and woke up with a start, sweating. I felt afraid and so undone. My mind began to race while I tried to decide the best course of action. I had gone over everything in my mind as to what I would do that day. In times past, I had met the probate judge and knew him to be a good man. I will just go talk to him, I thought. As a minister, I had visited people in the local psychiatric hospital. I told myself it was not a bad place. In all reality, it was similar to a prison, with locked doors and a schedule every day for the patients to follow. Here, he will get the help he needs, I continued to reason. I was trying to talk myself into going on to the courthouse. This was a hard decision for me to make. Should I, or should I not? This was the question I kept dealing with. I started the car and headed in the direction of the courthouse, still not fully convinced it was what I needed to do or, more importantly, what Chris needed. As I drove, I kept telling myself that this was the right thing to do. I felt I had no other choices. I forced myself to park the car in front of the county courthouse. I sat in the car for a while, looking at the front entrance. I don't even remember what I was looking at. Maybe I was embarrassed. I had heard of others having to do what I was about to do. One daughter who had her father committed told me how she felt at that time—how embarrassed she was. Yes, I was embarrassed.

I finally arrived in the office of the judge of probate and inquired as to what I needed to do in order to commit someone. The receptionist was very kind and ushered me into a private office to speak to someone about this matter. The lady who helped me understood my feelings. This was not her first time having to deal with this. I was greatly appreciative of her kindness and her helpfulness. She explained the law to me and gave me some papers to fill out. Having filled out all of the forms and with this lady going over them with me, I signed them. I would not let my wife or his wife sign any documents, not wanting Chris to blame them for the decision I had made. If someone needed to be blamed, it should be me. There was no need in him thinking his mom or wife had turned against him. Today, this was my responsibility, and I would have to deal with whatever came my way.

Chris stayed in the psychiatric unit at Jackson Hospital for five days. During that period of time, a diagnosis was given. No one had talked to me but said there was a diagnosis. None of us had ever discussed or even entertained the idea that Chris had bipolar disorder. I learned later in-depth what we were dealing with. This made it even more urgent to get him the proper care and on the proper medication.

Signing all of the documents before a notary, I departed the courthouse and returned to the hospital to pick up his mother. For a while, we did not discuss what I had done. We later talked about it and prayed and hoped this was the right decision.

The day came I had dreaded so long—his court date. I had to face him as being the one who was trying to have him committed. Chris had been assigned a lawyer, as I had by the court. We all took our places in the courtroom. His wife had asked about going. I did not think this was a good idea but did not try to stop her. What happened next, neither of us was prepared for.

Chris was led in with chains around his waist, shackled at the feet, and his hands cuffed to the chain around his waist. I was not ready for this. I did not know he would be treated as a criminal. I thought he would just walk in and take his place. There would then be procedures and questions. I was glad his mother decided not to come. I saw the look on his face as our eyes met. I smiled at him, trying to let him know I was there for him. But was I? Perhaps I was just being selfish and wanted someone else to deal with the problems we were having.

Court was called to order as the judge came in to take his place. A court reporter read why we were all there. It is not open court where people are allowed to sit and listen to the next case. It is only you and those who are part of the hearing. Different people take the stand. Questions were asked and answers were given. Finally, a witness—a nurse in charge of Chris's case from Jackson Hospital—was called to the stand. She was questioned by both lawyers. One lawyer, Chris's, tried to shake her testimony. He was presenting Chris's side, having already explained to him what these proceedings were for. She said, "Our diagnosis is Chris Brady is bipolar." This was the first time the word bipolar had ever been mentioned. In all the years we had been wrestling with these problems, this diagnosis had never been given. You may think me ignorant or just out of touch, but I knew little of mental illness. She explained the severity of the illness and why they had reached this conclusion. She explained what bipolar could do to an individual who remained untreated. Under severest cases, a person can even become a serial killer. The picture she painted was not a pretty one.

She was dismissed. I was called to the stand. That was the hardest thing I had ever done. I sat there and testified that my son was ill and should be locked up for a period of time until he was no longer a danger to himself. I could barely talk. I do not believe Chris was ever any danger to anyone but himself. He was always a joy when he was not sick or on drugs. One thing that had gotten better was his anger. He did not seem to have the anger he had as a teen.

Sitting on the stand, I looked at Chris. I was asked, "Why should Chris, your son, need to be committed?" I looked at Chris, and he looked at me, and I said to the court, to Chris, to his wife, "Chris doesn't know he needs help. I don't know what bipolar is." I looked Chris straight in the eyes and said, "I only know my son needs help, and I don't know how to give it to him." I looked at the judge and said, "Your Honor, I don't know where else to go. I don't know what else to do. My son has tried to commit suicide two times, and one day, he will succeed." Other questions were asked. My lawyer stayed away from the drug problem. I found out later why when the judge made his ruling.

His lawyer questioned me about Chris using drugs. "Has your son ever at any time used drugs?"

"Yes!"

"What is his drug of choice?"

"Crack!"

"You mean your son has a crack addiction?"

"Yes!"

"How bad is it? Once a day, once a week, how often does he take drugs?"

I did not know I was hurting our case with my answers. I thought we had a strong case.

Chris was called to the stand and shuffled to the chair, where he sat and looked out at the courtroom. He would not look at me directly but looked tired and somewhat distraught. However, he did look calm. I learned he had been put on medication and would need to take this medication or one like it for the rest of his life.

Chris took the stand, and the judge asked him if he had anything to say in his own defense. At first, he said no, but the judge changed his mind when he told him, "You better get to talking, son. You better convince me you do not need to be committed." Chris began to talk about different things. Things that were not relevant, but in the final analysis, it made no difference anyway.

The judge made his ruling. He began by saying how sorry he was for all these problems. Due to drugs being involved, he could not commit Chris. Even though a person is bipolar and even attempting suicide, the law would not allow him to commit an individual who was taking drugs. The testimony of the psychiatric nurse from the hospital was powerful; it made no difference, he said, because drugs were involved. The judge suggested several things that already had been tried, and I told him so.

"We have no more money to put him in a private facility," I told him. "He needs help," I said, "and we cannot give it to him." The decision had already been made. The law was clear.

The judge talked to me privately after court was dismissed and said how sorry he was, but his hands were tied by law. The chains were removed, and Chris returned home to an uncertain future for him and his family. We basically had run out of recourses, with no more money for treatment programs—programs that are expensive, leaving most people with few options as to what they can do.

The Brown house

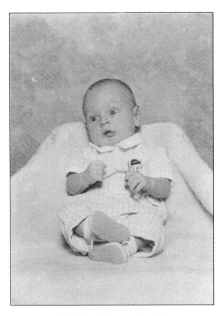

Chris, six weeks old

Chris helping plow the garden, riding on the handlebars

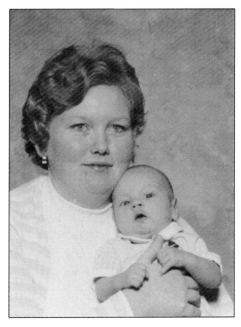

Betsy and Chris, at six weeks old

losing the son I didn't know

Big brothers look on while he enjoys second birthday cake

Chris and Michael

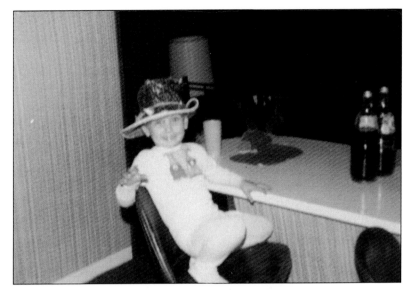

Chris sporting a cowboy hat

Chris in a Tom Thumb wedding while in kindergarten, wearing a tux

Fourth grade school picture

Chris in his Boy Scout uniform

In his military uniform

Chris's wedding day dressed in his tux

Celebrating second birthday with older son

On a fishing outing with his oldest son

Chris enjoying his favorite pastime, fishing

losing the son I didn't know

Family picture on the porch of Brown house at Thanksgiving

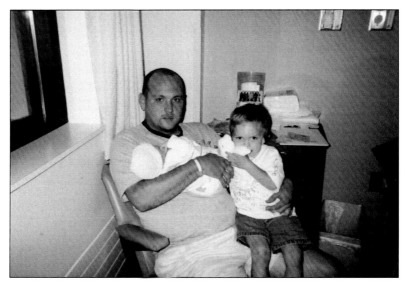

Holding his two children

The hillside on the Brady homeplace approaching the cemetery

Entrance to the Brady cemetery

losing the son I didn't know

The angel overlooking the cemetery

WE ARE NOT ALONE

Betsy and I, as time went on, found many families struggling every day with bipolar disorder. We were not alone in our struggles. Most people are able to live a normal life if they continue to take their medication, but mental illness is a disease that in times past would be swept under the rug. Families didn't want to deal with it, for they thought it was part of growing up. But it's not just rebellion. It's a serious illness that must be treated.

Bipolar, this was only a word to me. I had no clue. I learned there are many types of mood episodes with bipolar, as well as so many other symptoms. I began to do some reading about mental illnesses and began to see our son in these pictures. It was a disease we had been dealing with, which went undiagnosed for so many years.

For example, I always thought manic depression was something for serial killers. Thousands of people suffer with it. I continued to read and study, doing much research on the Internet and reading books to understand as much as we could.

Depression is another part of bipolar disorder that causes people to feel extremely sad for a long period of time. They do not have the desire to get out of bed or even eat. They lose interest in things they at one time enjoyed. Chris would spend days in bed. We would ask him if he was sick and would not receive an answer. He would have a faraway look in his eyes.

If someone in your family is suffering with depression, please do not overlook it. It will not get better. It is not temporary. Chris's depression often would last for days or weeks. Depression can be made worse by financial setbacks or problems within a relationship, such as breaking up with a girlfriend.

Mania is the other side of bipolar disorder. It may start with a good feeling, almost like a "high." Or it may make a person feel very irritable and angry. People with mania may do very risky things. This really scared us with Chris. As I mentioned earlier, the incident when he broke the window with his fist to get at his brother was only one incident in many. No amount of screaming or crying or discipline will stop them. We have watched Chris take great risks that would have made anyone else just cringe at the very idea.

Then there is hypomania, which is a milder form of mania. It can make people feel good. They may think they are getting more things done. An example of this is how Chris would get up in the morning, on occasions, and drive off to work singing, and in the evening, he would return depressed because he was not able to accomplish all he thought he could or should have. We have seen it time and time again. That "feel-good" stage would change into mania or depression. Hypomania is different from mania because it doesn't get in the way of things like work or family. It sometimes is not even noticed as a problem until it hits. There is also what is called "mixed mood." This is when feelings of mania and depression go back and forth quickly, sometimes even in the same day. With all types of extreme mood episodes, people are at risk for suicide. One extreme case of depression and mania happened one night when Chris was going down the road, and he decided, This is going to be the night. He tied off the steering wheel to where the car would go straight, accelerated to a high rate of speed, climbed over into the backseat, and laid down. We wondered, why did he not just hit a tree head-on? Why go to the trouble of tying the steering wheel and getting in the backseat? If he really wanted to kill himself, why do this? It made no sense to us. Those who were trying to rescue him from the car did not understand why he was in the backseat. None of it made any sense, but as I continued to read about mixed mood disorder, I began to understand a little bit more.

The car ran off the road and hit a tree, pinning him in the car, but the result was not what he wanted. Or was it? Perhaps it could have been a way of getting attention, some say. He was seriously injured, breaking his hip, which would take him a long time to get over. There were several operations, including hip replacement. That very morning, things were fine. You would think he was on the top of the clouds, and he changed that quickly. We as parents did not know how to recognize bipolar disorder. I had heard of manic depression, but not bipolar. I did not tie the two together until it was explained in court.

Bipolar disorder can be hard to detect because the symptoms can be similar to other mood disorders. Some people have the condition for ten years or more before a health care provider diagnoses it. If you think someone in your family may have bipolar—if they are experiencing any of the symptoms mentioned here—please do not overlook them.

When people are feeling manic or hypomanic, they are full of energy. They usually feel good. They feel "high on life" and don't always seek help. Sometimes they just cannot quit talking and feel like nothing can happen to them. I have the whole world before me. My life is good. This does not sound like an individual who has a disease.

On the other hand, people are more likely to seek help when they fall into depression.

> When people feel depressed, they are likely to describe only depression symptoms to their healthcare provider. In other words they do not tell the whole story because the only thing they see is depression. They may not mention the times when they are feeling "high on life," since depression is what they are feeling at the time. Therefore, it is common for a person to be incorrectly diagnosed with major depression instead of bipolar disorder. In fact nearly half of all patients who have bipolar disorder, sometimes called manic depression, will first be diagnosed with major depression. That's why it's important for people to say how they have been feeling weeks and even months before today to their healthcare provider in order to make it easier for the right diagnosis.
>
> Mental Illness Facts at www.NAMI.org

According to "What is Mental Illness: Mental Illness Facts" at www.NAMI.org, One person describes depression this way:

> I doubt completely my ability to do anything well. It seems as though my mind has slowed down and burned out to the point of being virtually useless. I am haunted with the total, the desperate hopelessness of it all. Others say, "It's only temporary, it will pass, you will get over it." But of course they haven't any idea of how I feel, although they are certain they do. If I can't feel, move, think, or care, then what on earth is the point?

In Chris's words, "I cannot control certain urges at certain times, like driving. My mind is saying, 'Drive fast! You must hurry up,' and the next thing I see are the blue lights in my mirror." We would always know when Chris was extremely depressed because he would sleep all the time, rarely getting up even to eat. He would sleep with his legs pulled to his middle. Our son Mike suffers from bipolar and is on medication. He, at times, will sleep around the clock and wake up irritable. As I said before, bipolar is inherited, and there are several members of my family who have it. My grandfather was a severe manic depressant, oftentimes treating his family harshly.

Chris had all the symptoms, such as increased energy level. Sometimes he thought he could move mountains. He would work from daylight to dark, like he was drinking some big energy drink. He had energy and needed only a little sleep. He could catch a small nap and be ready to go again. At times, he would stay up all night watching television and then go off to work.

This is part of mental illness that is hard to deal with. If an individual is on the right kind of medication, it slows the mind, and they are able to function, but off the medication, they become dangerous. There have been many cases where people who have come off the medication or never were on medication have killed their families or just walked into a store and started shooting. Their thoughts race, and they cannot make a decision rationally. Chris was easily distracted, even by minor things. At times, he would be talking about one thing, and then, all of a sudden, be distracted so easily by something of no consequence.

An article about bipolar disorder, by coincidence, was in the Montgomery Advertiser, our local newspaper, on September 20, 2005, the same day Chris's obituary appeared, titled "Bipolar Patients Benefit from Following Routine." For those who are suffering with this disease, this article should be helpful.

Patients suffering from bipolar disorder who underwent therapy to help them maintain a regular daily routine and cope with stress were able to avoid relapses over a two-year period, a study has found.

The study published in September's Archives of General psychiatry, examined a therapy developed by researchers at the University of Pittsburgh School of medicine.

Using what researchers dubbed the interpersonal and social rhythm therapy patients were taught how to keep to normal sleeping, eating, and other daily routines. They also were shown how to anticipate and cope with stress such as a diabetic who would be taught, for example, how to cook and eat differently.

"This is really a disorder characterized by massive disturbances in the body's clock and in all the things the body's clock controls," said Dr. Ellen Frank lead author of the study. "Their clocks need to be very carefully protected and we need to do everything we can to shore up and protect their fragile clock." Bipolar disorder, also commonly referred to as manic depression, is a brain disorder in which sufferers experience cycles of mania, depression or mixed states. Treatment for the disorder varies by patient, but often involves some type of medication combined with therapy.

Frank, a professor of psychiatry and psychology at the University of Pittsburgh School of medicine and Western psychiatric Institute and clinic, said doctors for years have counseled bipolar sufferers about managing their lives but no one had ever systematically put the information together. She said social rhythm therapy does that, and also teaches patients to identify the triggers in their relationships with other people that can cause relapses.

In this study, 175 patients suffering from the most severe form of bipolar were divided into several groups. All the patients were given medication for the disorder, along with some who received interpersonal and social rhythm therapy. The researchers found those who received therapy were more likely to not have relapses of their illness during a two-year maintenance phase.

Montgomery Advertiser article,
archives of general psychiatry
September 20, 2005

We had not known much about this kind of therapy. In our discussions, we found how it could have been helpful for Chris not only with managing bipolar but also his drug addiction. His drug addiction, according to his counselors, was brought about by the non-treatment of bipolar disorder. Due to our lack of knowledge, Chris was suffering from bipolar that went untreated for years. It only makes us wonder how many people, how many children and families, are suffering needlessly because they do not understand why they are acting the way they do. Would it have made a difference in Chris's life? Some say "No, it would have not changed the outcome." I do not believe this, for if managed correctly, I believe with all my heart that together we could have beat this disease, for we were like so many others, ignorant of what was going on in his mind.

WAKING UP A NATION

After Chris was released from the psychiatric unit, he returned to his wife. He began to get his life back in order. One day, the sheriff's department approached him to help catch some of the drug dealers he had been buying drugs from. This was right up his alley, for he liked anything that had adventure to it. Later, he would talk about how he had seen these things done on television but never dreamed he would have the opportunity to be an informant. An undercover deputy went with him to purchase drugs, but then Chris began bragging to others about what he was doing. Becoming too big of a risk, the sheriff's department would not allow him to go with them anymore. Good did come from his help, for due to some of this undercover work, at least two drug dealers were captured and sent to prison. But where one is arrested, there are hundreds more. Drug dealers are like a disease that cannot be cured.

This would not be the only time Chris would help the police find drug dealers. He always thought it was exciting. We questioned him about the dangers, but it was something he wanted to do.

Chris was arrested in a small town in south Alabama for possession of drugs. Working out a deal with the local police, he would not be charged if he would point out the drug dealer. It was a dangerous situation. Most drug dealers, in order to control their source, will go to any means—including murder—to protect their investments. His mother, without my knowledge, went with him one night to a secret location to meet with the police. Chris was an adult and could do what he wanted to do. I do not know what his mother thought she could do. They met with the police in a secluded cornfield outside of town on a dirt road. They came up with a plan and a strategy of how to catch the drug dealer. Our fear was that the drug dealer would get out of jail and come looking for Chris and find his family. This fear was realized when he got out of jail on bond and came looking for Chris. He was lucky he did not find him.

What is our government doing with local communities to eliminate drugs? During the Reagan days, there was the "Just Say No" campaign. People said this would not work; we needed to spend more time and money catching the drug dealers. I agree, they must be caught and sent to prison, where they cannot sell drugs. This is not the answer to a bigger and growing problem in our society. We must eliminate the need for drugs. Our children need to be taught abstinence. Our streets need to be cleaned up. We as a people—red, yellow, black, and white—need to quit fighting one another and start working together to create a better atmosphere for our children in which to live. This would lead to a more stable environment for the rearing of our children. Before we lose a generation, we must go to the source. If we eliminate the need, then we will be able to control the amount of drugs. Where there is no need, then the source will dry up. How can we do this? Far more intelligent people than me have contemplated this very thing. The late president Ronald Reagan addressed this issue and tried to implement the "Just Say No" program. After leaving office, this program was eventually dropped. We need to spend the money to eliminate drugs and create programs in our schools and our communities to teach and counsel those who are at risk. As long as we sit back and do nothing, there will be many situations like ours, and the cycle will never end. Families like ours will continue to stand by the grave of someone they love until we as a nation wake up.

The cycle continued when Chris went out one night and spent all the money he had made that week. He was out all night smoking crack. We received a call early the following morning from his wife. Chris had not come home, and she was worried. He arrived home before we got there. There was an argument between him and his wife. Someone called the police, who responded to a domestic disturbance. When we arrived, Chris was sitting in the back of the patrol car looking haggard. He really looked bad. I had not seen him look that bad in a long time. I almost cried. His mother had to get back in the car. His lips were toasted where he had been smoking crack all night.

At this time, his wife was pregnant with their first baby. It was a very difficult time for them. I talked to the police to find out what they were going to do. Chris had some outstanding warrants out on him, so they were going to take him in.

Betsy and I felt burdened. I wondered where it was going to end and when. I talked to the closest person to me, Jack Cates––my friend, my brother in Christ, my minister. Chris went to Jack and told him, "Uncle Jack, I want to quit. I want to do better, but I can't." He opened up and told him about his situations and how there seemed to be no answer for him.

This reminds me of a verse from the Bible that says, "Carry one another's burdens in this way you will fulfill the law of Christ" Galatians 6:2 (NIV). Carry one another's burdens! We had to rely upon people who loved us, even accepting financial help. I had been to Jack myself and unloaded on him. He prayed for God to give us the strength to get through this hurdle. Christians are to help one another. I found myself coming more to the foot of the cross and laying my burdens down because of this heavy burden.

Chris had warrants out for him, and he could not just leave town without settling with the court. I asked the police to allow me to help him so he would not have another charge on him. They said he would have to go in to satisfy the outstanding warrants but would not put any other charges against him if he agreed to get help. He was backed into a corner, and so were we. He agreed to get help. It was this or he went back to jail. Where was this help going to come from? He had no money, and neither did I. To keep him from going back to jail, we decided to check him back in a rehab center he had been in before. It would not be cheap. We did not know where the money would come from. First, I had to go to the police station and pay his outstanding warrants, which were almost $500. We were asked, "Why not let him go ahead to jail and be done with it?" Oh I thought about it! One side of me said to let him sit in jail, and the other side said he needed help. I paid the court the money he owed. This done, we made the one-hundred-mile drive to the rehab center, hoping we could strike a deal with them. The only deal we could make was for us to max out our credit cards and take a second mortgage on our house. This caused us to experience some of the most stressful times of our marriage, because we were in heavy debt. This was the only way we thought we could save Chris.

Many families have been placed in the same situation, trying to help, trying to save a family member. We do not blame the rehab centers. Many people are helped in these centers. They are expensive to operate, but there are so few for so many. There are programs for people, but where one is helped, there are many more who need help.

I have led many people on mission trips to the Republic of Panama. Sometimes we become so overwhelmed because of so many who come for the help and the services we offer. People come in with their family members, leading them by the hand, hoping that he or she will be healed. There are so many, and only a limited amount of surgeries can be performed. The healthcare provider becomes overwhelmed, for where one is treated, ten more are waiting in line. What are we to do?

One of the big problems with drug treatment and mental illness programs is there are too few programs and treatment centers for so many people. Those who give the treatments must then decide who they will be able to help. If a person has no money and there is no benefactor, they must do it alone. The crack habit can be broken, but is extremely difficult to do so.

According to myaddiction.com,

> The relapse rate for crack addiction is quite high. This is discouraging, but some users will require several rounds of treatment before clear progress is seen. One of the difficulties is that a return to crack seems like such an easy answer to problems with depression and anhedonia (an inability to feel pleasure). The drug seems like an instant cure.

Well-meaning people have said to me, "They made their decision, let them work it out." It is not easy to walk away from someone who so desperately needs help, nor is it biblical to do so. How does a person walk away or turn away from someone who needs help? Think about this: If it were up to another person to make a difference. What if that person were the only person who could help? What if a knock were to come on their door and opportunity looked them in the face to do something good? As each one of us looks at our Christian responsibly we know we can not pass by on the other side of the street.

Seeing someone stand beside the street as a Christian, as a parent, can we just pass on, saying, "It's not my problem"? It is my problem, for I live in this community, this town, the state, and nation. In order for things to be corrected, I must be part of the correction. We are often so judgmental when we see someone walking the streets, and maybe we might even be justified in our attitude, but how should we react? I have seen them, and so have you. We all have, and we nearly always pass by on the other side. With the high crime rate in our country, I can understand this, but let's be careful about branding these people and making unkind statements, such as "She is just a prostitute," or "He is a crack head or a dead beat." Maybe he or she is what you have just said. However, remember, this young person is someone's son or daughter, someone's family member, maybe a father or mother.

Until we began to deal with the problems with our son and understood why he did some of the things he did, I would pass by on the other side. It is so easy to judge an individual because of the clothes they wear or where circumstances find them. Sometimes, people are embarrassed when approached by someone begging and do not want to be bothered. We just look at them as if to say, "Don't bother me." I am not putting the guilt trip on you but hope we all will think about the problems within our communities around the country. Most all those we see are in the streets because of drugs, mental illness, or both. Jesus addresses this problem in the parable found in Luke 12 when a lawyer asked him the question, "Who is my neighbor?" It became even more personal when my son was one of those in the street looking for a buck. One preacher explained his realization this way: "The

Lord slapped me." Someone had to get his attention and bring him back around. Jesus is saying to people through this parable, "Wake up, and make a difference." Let's not say, "It's not my problem."

As we remember the story in the Bible about the priest, the Levite, and the Good Samaritan, perhaps we are reminded we have been guilty of this very act. Each one passed by a stranger and all saw the same thing—someone needing help. Two of these people thought it was not their responsibility and passed by on the other side of the road while the Samaritan saw a responsibility and took it upon himself to make a difference. It is our responsibility. We live in the United States of America, one of the youngest countries in the world, and yet too many of us are passing by on the other side of the road, unwilling to help with this growing problem.

"I don't know what to do," is generally the answer people give. Or "It does not affect me and my family. Therefore, it is not my responsibility." Far too long, we as a people have failed to get involved. The salvation of our youth is my personal responsibility. It is your responsibility. We cannot continue passing by on the other side of the road and neglecting the hurting.

Someone said, "I will tell you what needs to be done. Round all of the crack heads and the prostitutes up and throw them in jail, where they need to be." Let's suppose we go out and round up all of the crack heads and throw them in jail. I will say to you, go back the next day, the next night, and there are more who have taken the place of those who were locked up. Those who were locked up will be right back on the street as soon as they are released, usually the next day. This is not the way to handle a growing problem in our society. Each one of us must help in our community. We must become involved some way, somehow, with local governments and with local organizations to help save the youth of our nation. There are some who are trying to make a difference, such as inner-city ministries throughout the country. These are great organizations crying out for volunteers.

One organization I came in contact with from Denver, Colorado, called "Crossbones," was going into the streets, getting the young people, and bringing them in and trying to teach them about a better way of life. They did not judge them by the way they dressed or the length of their hair. They did not care how many piercings or how many tattoos they had; they were only interested in the salvation of that person. They did not immediately begin preaching to them but gave them some things to think about. Things such as how Jesus could make a difference in their lives.

We must become involved in the lives of the children of our nation. From this generation comes the next generation of leaders. We must not walk by on the other side of the road like the priest and the Levite did.

As parents, we tried to make a difference in Chris's life by not turning him away. It was not always easy and not always pleasant. What else could we have done? Remember, God does not love the sin but the sinner. Where does that leave you and me? When our son was one of the deadbeats, we were grateful for those kind people who helped him.

Betsy and I decided we did not care if we lost everything; we were going to make every effort to get him the help he so desperately needed. This was now past him begging on the street or wallowing in his vomit in a crack house. We paid for what he needed, but in the end, it was not enough.

Chris was in counseling, where people are paid to listen and to give good advice. He desperately needed help, and we as parents did not know how to give it to him. Chris was now doing better and was responding to treatment. He was, as his counselors told us, "doing well and making a lot of progress." His wife had agreed to go to the rehab office in Birmingham to receive counseling as well. She needed to learn how to live with and to help someone who had an addiction. She arrived and was about to begin class when her water broke and she went into labor. She was transported to the hospital by ambulance.

Chris was notified and brought to the hospital by the staff of the center. We all arrived about the same time. Chris, as the father, was allowed to go back with his wife and stay and watch his son's birth. It was a long wait, and sometime during the early morning, Chris came through the doors carrying his son wrapped in a blanket. He stood there looking at all of us. He was not smiling as a happy father should be. Perhaps he knew the reaction of some standing in the group, and so he was afraid. His wife's family was also there. All waited anxiously to see the baby. Chris did not let us see him. He kept him wrapped up. He said to all of us, "Before you look at him, you need to know he has some problems. But the doctor says there is nothing here that cannot be fixed." We gathered around him, and he pulled back the blanket. We looked down into the face of a child who was deformed. He had a gap from his lip up into his nose cavity. His head was flat on one side, and his left ear had just a piece of flesh hanging there. But everything else was normal. There were ten fingers and ten toes, and he was sleeping so peacefully, all wrapped up in the arms of his father. I do not believe Chris ever saw a deformed child; others did and blamed him. Chris never did treat this child as though something was wrong. He loved him with a love we read about in the Bible—with a love that looked through deformity, ugliness, and imperfection.

There were those there who began to say, "Drugs, that's what caused him to be so deformed." The doctor immediately said, "No, drugs did not cause this. He has a disease called Goldenhar syndrome. It will take many operations, but he can live a normal life."

The heartbreaking part of the story for Chris and so many others like him is although they love their family, it seems they have no control over their bodies. It does not always mean people who take drugs are bad parents. They have no control, for the drugs control every thought and every motive to the point they will allow their family to go hungry and without a place to live so they can satisfy their habit.

We all know people who smoke. Smokers do not realize it, but they have no consideration for others. Many will even say they are being discriminated against and should be allowed to enjoy their cigarettes anywhere they want to. Other people's health is not their concern. However, when one quits smoking, or some other bad habit, they understand why people felt the way they did.

Very few people understand mental illness, and this misunderstanding leads to harmful attitudes toward those who are sick. As we watched our son wrestle day after day, we felt so useless. Chris was at the very height of his drug usage when he went into the rehab before his son was born. When he was born, we were in hopes that this was going to be the very thing that would cause him to be able to break the habit and also learn how to control his mental illness. This is another mistaken attitude people who live with this disease every day have. Just because something good comes into their lives does not mean it will change anything. Yes, sometimes it gives them something to work for, something to look forward to. It does give them a reason to get better, but it does little to cure a person's disease.

He began taking medication for bipolar disorder, but the medication was very expensive, and few can afford it without the help of insurance or someone who would give it to them. A nurse practitioner from Long Beach, Mississippi, began to give Chris samples of the medicine he needed to control his disease. He began to do well and, under counseling, was able to cope with both bipolar and a crack addiction. At last, he began to respond favorably to treatments.

Having gotten bipolar disorder under control, he and his wife had to make some very difficult and hard choices. It was decided for him that to be able to quit drugs, he would need to move his family out of the Montgomery area, even out of the state. We wanted so much to see our son whole again, for it had been years, and it had taken a toll on us. Counselors say one way to help someone addicted to drugs is to move away where no one knows them and start over again.

A drug dealer from whom Chris had purchased drugs in times past left some crack in the door of his house, which is a temptation almost no drug addict can resist. Chris was trying to go straight, staying away from drugs. We would not let anyone know where they were living, but somehow, the drug dealer found out. Moving was his only recourse. This is not always easy to do, but at this point, we felt we had to help him in a last-ditch effort to save him and his family.

This disease, coupled with the drugs, controlled our every thought and our every moment. When it was decided they would move to Springfield, Missouri, to begin a new life, we were ecstatic. Betsy and I went with Chris and his family to Springfield to look around and help them find a place to live.

People asked, why Springfield, Missouri? Chris was a big fisherman, almost professional. He had purchased an old boat and was fixing it up. He would fish often, practicing all of the time, learning new techniques and the best way to catch the big fish. While living in Springfield, he spent a lot of time at the Bass Pro Shop and met one of the biggest professional fishermen who appeared on television often. He and Chris became good friends, and he would call Chris and ask him to go practice with him for a tournament, which he was always glad to do. This fisherman gave Chris all kinds of equipment and clothes. Chris was happy. Perhaps the happiest we had ever seen him. He loved Springfield. It seemed he was going to be able to kick the habit and live a normal life. He continued to take his medication to control his mental illness, and for the first time, he was free of drugs and had been clean for several months. For the first time, he felt he could kick the habit. And so did we.

There was, however, the thought in the back of our minds of his counselor, who said to him, "Chris, you must remember that you are a drug addict, a crack head, and abuser of drugs." He was very blunt, but he had to understand this very important fact: once a crack head, always a crack head. "You must remember this. One day, when you least expect it, you are going to be hit with an urge for drugs. It's going to hit you hard. It might be six months or two years, but it will hit you, and you must decide now what you are going to do when the urge hits. You must continue counseling wherever you go and attend the Narcotics Anonymous meetings."

He and his family began attending a church in the city and participating in the worship services. We were so proud of his accomplishments. They made new friends. Friends that even today will call us and tell us how they remember Chris and his family and ask about his children. He occupied himself with his hobbies and work while taking a lot of time with his wife and son. They would often go camping. Chris would put a life preserver on his young son and take him riding in the boat. Chris became such an avid fisherman, which became therapy for him. In order to control a drug habit, one must find something else to put in place of using drugs—something else that would bring him more happiness.

Chris told us he never got over the desire for drugs. He said during this period of time, he would contemplate where he could find drugs in Missouri and, at times, think about going and looking for them.

He was able to fill his life with going to church and taking time with his family. They developed a good relationship with a man who owned a lawn mower shop nearby. Chris would go there and tinker with the mowers and learn how to work on them. This friendship would be the best thing that could have happened to Chris and gave him something else to take the place of drugs.

Chris tried different kinds of work, mostly in the yard and landscaping business and did well for a period of time, but this time, he could not control his mind. Sometimes he would not finish a job before going somewhere else or meeting up with friends or going fishing. Part of mental illness, depending what one has, is not being able to finish a task. With the mind racing, one cannot finish projects and jumps from one thing to another. Many people deal with this part of mental illness called attention deficit disorder, or ADD. This caused him many problems, even causing him to lose his business.

He decided to go to truck driving school and learn how to drive the big rigs. Again, he found something he was good at, learning fast. It was not long until he was on the road. He made good money, and they were happy to have things they had not had for a long time. He drove back and forth from California and enjoyed seeing new places. For Chris to be satisfied, he always had to have something exciting going on. He had to stay focused on the moment. He would relate to us that his desire for drugs was always there. He knew they were close by, all he had to do was ask the right people and he could go get them.

A Phone Call

Chris had been clean for two years and began to experience some problems. Hoping to help him through them, Betsy and I decided to go to Missouri, making the twelve-hour drive often. This would be a very critical time. If he could get over this hurdle, maybe he would get a reprieve for two more years. I do not know exactly what brought it all on. Perhaps it was an argument with his wife or a problem at work. These occurrences were a normal part of life, but for a person who constantly deals with substance abuse, it can be devastating. We did not know exactly what happened. We reminded him of the words of his counselors, "It will hit you when you least expect it."

We got a call one day from him while he was in New York City making a delivery. I joked with him later that driving in New York City in a car was enough to cause a person to have a heart attack, but to drive a tractor-trailer there was something else. I also reminded him of the time he and his friend drove to downtown New York when only fourteen. His reply was, "I was stupid then."

Chris was taking his medication to control his mental illness, and it was always a challenge to keep him with the medication. At that point, we were no longer able to get the medication free. He now had insurance that would pay for part of it, but while in New York, he ran out of his medication. He had been without, even before he got to New York. Fortunate for him, he was using a pharmacy that had stores throughout the United States. Being without the medication brought about flu-like symptoms, and he said that he could not control his thinking and wanted to just park the truck and go to sleep. He did this on one occasion, and someone noticed the truck had been sitting in a rest area for a long period of time, and the police checked on it and found him sleeping. He slept around the clock. He was extremely depressed. We helped him get enough medication by going to a local pharmacy in Montgomery and paying for the drugs there while he went to the pharmacy in New York and picked it up. He later would relate to us as he called us upon his departure from New York, "I see New York in my mirrors, and that's the last time I plan on coming back." The time clean of drugs was short for Chris.

I don't know when he began to use drugs again. There were many things we chose just not to know, but it was always on our mind. After his son was born, Betsy and I went to Springfield at least once a month. This was a critical time for his family, for his son was undergoing some very serious operations. He had already had several operations to repair the cleft lip and palate and was doing well. He did not even look like the same little boy we saw that day in the hospital. We remembered the words Chris had related to us from the doctor, "There is nothing here that cannot be repaired."

He had to undergo a series of operations on his neck. He was born with his head bent over and could not straighten his neck, so the doctors in Missouri decided to cut some of the muscles and ligaments to bring his neck straight. This was a very successful operation, and he began to take on the look of a normal child. He was such a joy to be around and loved his Grammy, always jumping up and down when we would pull up in the driveway. Every month, we would make the drive on Friday evening after work and leave Sunday afternoon after church for the return trip home.

Chris continued to desire drugs. I knew it was on his mind a lot. He was having problems focusing. This could have been a combination of drugs and bipolar disorder. I told him, "Son, when you have this urge, please call me or call someone very close to you. Spend time with your family, and do the things you enjoy doing. Use all the will power you can muster. Do not go back to drugs." Shortly before his death on Friday morning, when I knew he was struggling with so much on his mind, I said almost the same thing to him. "Call me, son. Call me, please. Wherever you are, regardless of the time, call me."

It would not be enough. The urge, the craving, was too great for him to overcome. If Chris ever stopped calling his mother, he was having a problem. He always called her every day, even when on the road. Betsy would say, "Chris has not called today." She then would get on the phone and call him. Sometimes she would get him, and sometimes she would not.

He went out in search of drugs, and it did not take him long to find them. No one knew for a time, for he was able to keep it covered up until the drug usage got worse.

He had taken his wife and son on a trip with him in his big rig. His son loved to sit in his dad's big rig. Leaving his family at the hotel where they stayed, he got up to search for drugs. He found them at a local truck stop. The drugs continued, and things began to go downhill from there. Chris fell, and he kept on falling!

He lost his driver's license due to unpaid tickets, and during this time, his wife would become pregnant with their second child. They were beginning, however, to have more struggles with money, and it was affecting their relationship. His wife was working in Springfield with a good job, but was having problems trying to balance everything. Betsy flew out to Springfield to help them, but she also was working and could not spend all of her time there. We also had other grandchildren we needed to spend time with. Not only was Chris having problems with his mental illness and drugs, but he was in constant pain from a broken hip he received in a suicide attempt a couple of years earlier. It popped all the time when he walked, so he had to take pain medication, which is not good for someone who is a recovering drug addict. The pain became so intense that he underwent hip replacement surgery. He recovered fully from this and was able to return to the road.

His drugs, coupled with family problems, caused much stress on his family. They decide to return to Alabama and moved to Geneva County. Over the next year, he jumped from one trucking company to another, and his problems in his family got worse. His drug usage was increasing, and he was having severe bouts with depression. Things went from bad to worse until his wife left him and returned to Montgomery.

There were several court hearings in Geneva over child visitation. During this time, he and his wife divorced. It has been said that people who divorce find it harder to get over than the death of a family member. It is often hard to move on. His problems continued to increase while we tried to help find solutions. We did not know what to do or how to help him. Over the next several months, we went through many stressful times. We arranged visitation with his children and helped where we could.

Chris decided the best thing for him to do was to return to Missouri, where he had friends and could obtain work. It was hard on us to try to make sure he saw his children. The problems began to increase with his drug usage, and his bipolar condition was out of control. He could not afford the medication and wasn't taking any.

AS WE STRUGGLE

Returning to Missouri by himself, Chris passed through Birmingham, pulling a boat loaded down with everything he owned. If the circumstances had been different, it would have been funny, for the scene reminded us of a redneck traveling down the highway pulling a junk trailer. He decided to stop at McDonald's on the north side of the city to use the restroom and get something to drink. This was not a good side of town to be on, but this never bothered Chris. As he was pulling out of the parking lot, a police cruiser was pulling in and decided to check Chris out. This was one time Chris was clean and had broken no laws, but I suppose he looked suspicious, and being the time of night it was, they turned on the blue lights. He panicked and took off, traveling south on I-65 with the police in chase. By this time, many police——as well as the county district attorney—had joined in the chase. The chase was on TV and heard by family members, who lived sixty miles away. He was not traveling very fast because of the load he had on the boat and he was going up the mountain. He ran out of gas and pulled over, only to jump out and make a run for it. He was tackled and tased by the police. They thought he was either high on drugs or drunk, but neither was the case. He tested negative for both when placed in the county lockup.

Fleeing from the police is a very serious offense. Depending on what charges were filed, he could have received a heavy fine, as well as jail time. I was out of the country, and his mother was recovering from surgery but went to Birmingham to bail him out of jail. When asked why he ran, because the law had nothing on him, he said, "My mind said 'run,' and it seemed I had no other choice. I don't know why I ran." After he was released from jail on bond, he continued on to his destination to Missouri.

He did not return to Birmingham for his court hearing, and a bench warrant was issued for his arrest. For several months he avoided arrest—until one day, he was stopped by local police in Missouri. He was found to have outstanding warrants from Birmingham and was placed in the local city jail until the district attorney was notified to see if he wanted to extradite him back to Birmingham. Chris waived extradition, and the district attorney sent a unit to pick him up. He spent the next forty-some-odd days in jail waiting for trial because he had jumped bond. This was one time we could not help him get out. We did go to all of his hearings and had several conversations with his lawyer. The charges were serious, and the district attorney would not reduce them to a lesser offense nor let him out of jail. He was in on the chase, and this person was going to pay for his crime.

While in jail, Chris had much time to think. In his own words, he said, "I was somewhat rejuvenated and felt maybe I could make a difference, even if it's through words." He wrote the following paper. He had his Bible with him and understood a lot about the Bible, and as you will see, he was very intelligent. Betsy had often said, "As intelligent as Chris was, he could have been a millionaire. If only." There were many "if onlys." As one can see from the following article, he could think and reason. He also had much to offer.

> When people say, "Life is hard," I always think to myself, Well, of course, it is. I am sure we can all identify with that saying, "Life is hard." The path God takes us on sometimes leads us away from what we think is good for us, causing us to think we missed a road or took a wrong turn. God's goodness doesn't always translate into a life free of trouble. God's love often leads us down roads that are uncomfortable. Paul said in Philippians 1:29, "To you it has been granted on behalf of Christ, not only to believe in him, but also to suffer for his namesakes."
>
> In Deuteronomy 32:11–12, God is portrayed as a dedicated mother eagle trusted by her young, even in the scary experience of their learning to fly. A mother eagle builds a comfortable nest for her young, padding it with feathers from her own breast. The God-given instinct that builds secure nest also forces the eaglets out of it before long. Eagles are made to fly, and the mother eagle will not fail to teach them. Only then will they become what they are meant to be. God is our mother eagle teaching us what we need to be through our trials and struggles.
>
> Few men and women can fulfill their hopes and plans without some interruptions or disappointments along the way. Man's disappointments are often God's appointments, and the things we believe are tragedies may be the very opportunities through which God has chosen to show his love and grace. In the end, we will become better and stronger Christians than if we carried out our own plans. Remember the Lord's promise in Psalm 84:11, when he said, "No good thing will be withheld from those who walk up rightly."

A poem I read says it best:

Then trust in God to all the days
Fear not for he doth hold thy hand;
Though dark thy way, still singing in praise;
Sometime, sometime, we'll understand.

Life sometimes makes demands on us we do not want to bear. Yet, the most unjust and pointless suffering is an opportunity for us to respond in a way that our Lord can turn us into his own likeness. We can take joy in our trials. We know adversity is working to make us perfect and complete, lacking nothing. You remember these are the words of James 1:3–4. But this often takes time. We want the quick fix, but there are no shortcuts that can accomplish God's ultimate goal and purpose for us. The only way to grow in Christ's likeness is to submit each day to the conditions God brings into our lives. Progress is inevitable. I read a story of a man who took home a cocoon so he could watch the moth grow. As the moth struggled to get through the tiny opening, the man enlarged it with a snip of his scissors. The moth came out easily, but its wings were shriveled. The struggle through the narrow opening is God's way to force fluid from his body into its wings. The merciful snip in reality was cruel. Sometimes the struggle is exactly what we need to become what God intends us to be.

A minister was addressing a group of men. He took a large piece of paper and drew a black dot in the center and held it up and asked them what they saw. One person replied, "I see a black dot." The complete silence prevailed. "What else do you see?" was the question. Silence prevailed. The speaker said, "I'm surprised; you've overlooked the most important part—the sheet of paper." We are often distracted by disappointments, and we are prone to forget the innumerable blessings we receive from the Lord.

I heard a saying, "As you travel down life's pathway, keep your eye upon the doughnut and not upon the hole."

Rather than concentrating on the trials of life, we should fix our attention on its blessings. Let's say with the psalmist, "Blessed be the Lord who daily loads us with benefits" (Psalm 68:19). Spend your time counting your blessings, not airing your complaints.

Why is sin so bad? When I found this question in some study material I was reading, the first thing I thought of was pain. That is exactly why sin is so bad because it causes so much pain. Horrible, excruciating pain. Unrelenting, unbearable, unspeakable pain. With every slash across Jesus' back, and with every muscle-burning step up Golgotha's hill, our Savior received the punishment for our sin. In our "let's make everything okay" world, we often look at sin and wonder, What's the big deal? After all, our sin is not so bad. If we lie a little or cheat a bit, what's the harm? Our needs cannot be met until our sin problem is overcome. For this reason, Christ rode into Jerusalem on a donkey with his face set toward the cross, knowing full well the shameful and painful death he would suffer there. Our sins were the reason for the torment Jesus suffered as he made his way to the cross, and he hung on the cross and died a terrible death. We can never undo what has been done. Jesus's pain cannot be reversed. But we must understand if we knowingly continue to sin, we are turning our back on Jesus and his pain. It is like saying it doesn't matter what we put Jesus through, we're going to do what we want. To sin in light of the cross is to tell Jesus that even his intense suffering has not taught us about the awfulness of sin.

Paul gives us the remedy in Romans 8, when he said that through the forgiveness of Christ, we are freed from eternal condemnation. Then by the strength of the dwelling of the Holy Spirit, we are empowered to do the will of God, and someday, in heaven, these mortal bodies of ours will be redeemed. Praise God! Christ broke the power of sin. We can serve him in newness of life. To overcome sin is to starve the old nature and feed the need.

We need to strive to be like Christ. We are to love and help others, for we are God's hands on earth, created both to receive help and give it. First John 3:17 says, "Whosoever sees his brother in need, and shuts up his heart from him, how does the love of Christ abide in him?" To be Christians, we must always be willing to obey his Word. We have to lead by example. What an honor to bear a name linking us to God's son. Our Savior and Redeemer! This should shape and mold our manner of living so it becomes increasingly consistent with the way Jesus spoke and conducted himself. We have a noble calling. Let's always keep in mind whom we are. Let God's love shine in us so we can experience God's love. If we want to call ourselves Christians, let's live up to our name.

I've been a Christian all of my adult life, and I have been on a roller coaster ride. God has been trying to work in my life all these years, and I have blocked him out. Even when God has saved my life and healed me from afflictions, I thanked him but eventually turned away again. How many times has this happened to me? I was once in a car accident and received serious injuries, all because of my stupidity. I got a broken hip that would plague me for the rest of my life, causing several operations. For some reason, I did not die in that accident that night. Sitting here in this jail, I wonder why. Why did I survive? I suppose that God has something else for me. Perhaps he gave me more time to think about my life, but whatever it was, I sit here in this jail cell. In a six-by-nine jail cell I wrote this lesson and reflected upon my life. I turned my life back over to God. God had me cornered, and this time, there was no more Mama and Daddy. There were no brothers to pay me out of trouble, just my heavenly Father and myself. I began to think, This has got to be hell on earth. Then I thought about heaven and my eternal life. Heaven or hell! That scared me. I changed my life tonight, sitting here in this jail cell. We all need to think, Where is our eternal life going to be spent?

Being incarcerated, I befriended a young man much younger than me. His name was Jason, and he was nineteen years old. He had been in jail for twenty-five months. He was seventeen when he was arrested for murder. Jason began using drugs at the age of nine, harder drugs by the age of twelve, and in jail for the first time by the age of thirteen ; eventually, he was arrested and convicted of capital murder at the age of seventeen . He was sentenced to life without parole and would never again see outside of a prison wall. As we talked, he said, "It's over. I have nothing to live for, but I just keep going."

I told him he had a lot to live for. There are two kinds of life without. Life without parole and eternal life without heaven. It made him think. I still correspond with Jason in hope of his baptism someday. We all need to think about this. I want an eternal life in heaven. God is there to help each step of the way. Let's do our part, but as with many, we have to take the first day.

—Chris Brady

These are Chris's words during his final time in jail. I believe them to be honest and sincere words of someone crying out, "I need help, for I cannot walk it alone." Children, regardless of their age, are still our children, and as they become accountable for their actions, they must pay the price for what they have done, but they should never be cast aside as though they were not important.

Chris had many struggles in life that led him down the wrong pathways and ultimately to his death. Even with extreme difficulties, Chris had a good heart. He was a good person. It is hard for me to write of the direction his road took him. To write about the bad and not show the good or the potential he had would not be fair to Chris. This would only make people see Chris as just another rotten egg or another bad apple in the barrel. I do not want people who read this book to think Chris was all bad. He wasn't always in jail or trying to find drugs. People need to know he was a good person with a good heart. Living is sometimes like making a movie. We need to look behind the scenes. Looking behind the scenes of Chris's life, not only do we see the mistakes he made but also all the good he did.

If people who knew Chris were truthful, they would have to admit he was always kind, speaking respectfully. Many times, he would go out of his way to help others. He worked for people he knew could not pay him and did not ask for anything.

While living in Missouri, he participated in church and was respected by the members. Being a good father while clean was part of who he was. He loved his children with a passion. Camping, going fishing, and going to Waffle House to eat were part of a weekly life. To this day, his oldest son loves going to Waffle House, so we take him on special occasions.

Someone once said, "Bring your flowers now, for one day, it will be to late. Tell a person you love them now, for one day, you will regret it." At his funeral, people I knew who had spoken so harshly about him, even passing judgment on him, came up to me and his mother and said good things about him. I am not saying they were not being honest in what they had to say. The point is, if you have something good to say about someone, say it now, not at the funeral. Good words, kind words, oftentimes will change the course of one's life. I place the blame nowhere and on no one for the outcome of this tragedy. It was just that—a tragedy. I myself am guilty of not always saying what was in my heart. When you know a person is struggling in life, it might be your word of encouragement that will be the words needed to change the course of their life.

As a Christian, is this not biblical to speak good and not evil? The Bible says, "Let your words be with grace seasoned with salt."

As we know, salt makes food taste better. So it is with kind words. They make people feel like living. People respond to kindness and words of encouragement.

Chris was kind and considerate when all was going well. There were long periods of time when things did go well. He would stop and help people who were stranded. He picked up people and helped them get on their way. He cut people's grass for free. Talking to him, one would not have had a clue that standing before them was someone headed for self-destruction. Let's never forget that just because a person is mentally ill or a drug addict does not mean they are bad people.

Each one of us can learn lessons from others. Never reach a point where you think you cannot learn. "What can a drug addict teach me?" you may ask. Looking back over the course of Chris's life, I see so many things I have learned. I moved on with life wishing I had done some things differently. What would those things have been? Look for the good. Do not always focus on the bad. Sometimes in a beautiful bouquet of flowers all we see is the one wilted flower. We fill our lives concentrating on the bad when there is so much good to think about. We remember the hurricane but not the sunshine that followed; the accident but not the recovery. Our prayers are filled with request but limited in thanks to God for all the good things.

After Chris's death, Betsy and I sat on our porch and talked of all the good Chris had done, even looking at the flowerbed he so proudly made for us—a flowerbed all the way across the front of our house that we care for, even after all these years. We leave it there to remind us of the good things in his life. "Hey, Pop, look at that piece of art." Those words are forever embedded in my mind. I still plant the same kind of flowers each spring to display his work of art. One person who never spoke unkindly to him was his mother. I am guilty, but not Betsy.

The Love of a Mother

Betsy's love as a mother in everything I have written thus far brings much emotion from me. I watched her, as a mother, nurture our children as no one but a mother would have done. We all know there's nothing greater than the love a mother has for her children. We have heard of mothers dying for their children and taking great risk to rescue them when in danger. Betsy gave up so much for our children, even doing without things she needed so she could provide more for them. I also watched the love Chris had for his mother. He had a great love for me as his father, but there's just something different about Mom.

Watching young men play football or other sports, all of a sudden, the camera is on one of them and they say, "Hey, Mom." Sick children always call for their mom. This is natural and is as it should be. God put in moms a love that we fathers do not understand. On another note, Chris would say to his mom, "The two best men I know are Daddy and my uncle Jack." I remember those words today, and they mean a lot to me. Although he loved me, we did not have the closeness he and his mother had. I suppose this was because he knew she understood him and would not judge him so harshly. Chris never forgot his mother. He would call her every single day, without exception. If he did not call, she would always say, "Something is wrong."

In 2008, when Betsy and I were on our way back from Nebraska, we decided to go through Missouri to visit a friend of Chris's. He was an older man who had befriended him when no one else would. He had given him an opportunity to help him in his lawn mower shop. He often advised him about situations he was facing.

We stood there in his shop and talked about the times he shared with Chris while he lived in Missouri. During our conversation, he said, "Chris loved you so much," and became very emotional when he looked at Betsy. Standing in his shop, we could not help but shed the tears we had been holding back, although it had been almost three years since his death. Betsy would leave after work on Friday and drive all night so she could be with them just for the weekend and be back at work on Monday. She knew he was struggling and felt being there for this short time might make the difference.

I know beyond a shadow of a doubt it was his mother who kept him alive those last few years. She sat on our back porch and took the time to listen to him, even though it was the same story over and over again.

After he and his family had moved back to Geneva, Alabama, he was experiencing marital difficulties and separated. He had not seen the children in a while. Betsy knew the struggles he was having and the deep depression he was in. She amazed me beyond anything I had ever seen. If God ever put a caring mother on this earth, it was her. It was getting to where Chris could not get through the day without some form of assurance from his mom.

He was preparing to drive his tractor-trailer to South Carolina to pick up a load. As we talked, with his big rig parked in front of his house, a look of despair was written all over him. It was all I could do to sit there and talk to him. This was unlike other times when he would turn on the charm or fake his entire feelings to get money, gas, or even a pack of cigarettes. He could not concentrate or focus. He was smoking one cigarette after another and shaking. His ashtray was running over, and I said very gently, "Chris, how can I help? I know something is going on." I am 100 percent convinced if it had not been for his mother that day, Chris would have ended it all that very day.

Looking back, I saw this again the day he died. I just did not put it all together because I was in a hurry to leave for a speaking engagement.

Betsy sat there and tried to figure it all out. She knew something was wrong. She would not leave him. He told us he had to take a load to South Carolina and also pick up another load to bring back. I had to be selfish and did not want Betsy to go, but she said, "He cannot go by himself, and maybe this will give me a chance to talk to him." I was reluctant but agreed. It did not matter whether I agreed or not, she had made up her mind and was going.

She packed her bag and got in the truck to ride with him as to protect him. This was her son, and she could see in his eyes something was wrong. She could see things that I could not see—that no one could see—and she knew he was not doing well emotionally.

Upon their return a few days later, she said she had learned one thing: "Chris could definitely drive a tractor-trailer." She said to watch him back it up to the dock was amazing. By the time they returned, he was doing better and seemed to be settling down. The best medicine he had on that trip was riding with him.

On another occasion, when he was struggling for money and living by himself, she went to the house where he was living and helped him bale pine straw so he could make a little money. This was very hard on her, but she did it. I asked her, "Why not go home for a while?" Her reply to me was, "You don't think I know how to work?" She helped him rent a trailer to deliver all the way to Montgomery. Betsy never could say no.

I am at loss for words to describe the love and compassion that came from her. I watched her spend her last dollar to help him, even when she knew it would not work, but she was always there. It reminds me of what Solomon said in Proverbs 31: "Her price is far above rubies."

Mothers and wives are special people, and I, for one, have never been able to give them the proper credit. Betsy had the disposition all mothers should have, and our home became a safe haven—a place where our children could always return. With no place else to go and nowhere to turn, Chris knew the one place always open to him was our home. Sometimes, when I would be so frustrated and would have rather closed the door and said, "Go somewhere else," his mother would never do that. She never did turn her back on any of her children. Even today, as a grandmother, when our grandchildren want to come over, she never says no, even when she isn't feeling well. She has always emphasized, "The home is a place of safety, a place of refuge, and should always be open to our children."

THE HOME;
A SAFE PLACE

Always take attempted suicide seriously. I have heard people say, "I don't believe so-and-so wanted to kill themselves. He or she was just trying to get attention." Maybe, but understand, whether it be for attention or whether it is a failed attempt, please take it seriously. I have made some of the same statements, saying, "He was not really serious, for if he had been, he would not be with us today."

The following information came from www.NAMI.org. Those of us who are dealing with children with illnesses don't understand but must attempt to educate ourselves on what we are dealing with.

> The most dangerous and fear-inducing features of bipolar disorder are the self-harm behaviors and potential for suicide. An estimated 10 percent kill them selves. Deliberate self-harming (cutting, burning, hitting, head banging, hair pulling) is a common feature of bipolar disorder. Individu-

als who self harm report that causing themselves physical pain generates a sense of release and relief which temporarily alleviates excruciating emotional feelings Some individuals with bipolar disorder also exhibit self-destructive acts such as promiscuity, bingeing, purging and blackouts from substance abuse. It is important for the individual, family, and clinician to be able to draw a distinction between the intent behind suicide attempts and self-injurious behaviors. Patients and researchers frequently describe self-injurious behavior as a means of reducing intense feelings of emotional pain. Some data suggest that self-injurious behavior in bipolar disorder patients doubles the risk of suicide attempts.

In Chris's case, we saw some of the symptoms, such as binging, doing harmful things to himself, and even at times to those around him. He later would not even remember having done some of these things. He had said many times what he wrote in his suicide letter, "Life is not worth living." He also said things like, "I don't care if I die. I would be better off dead." People with bipolar disorder who have not received treatment or do not stay on their medications often become suicidal. This problem gets deeper as one goes on. They feel rejected by those who love them the most, which then will lead to drug addiction and despair. The despair leads to loneliness. Drug addicts often feel so terribly alone. They are in a world of destruction, often with no place to go.

Young people on our streets are searching for a place to go, addicted to drugs, rejected by family and community. No one will have anything to do with them, and so they search. What they find is a drug dealer or pimp who will use them until they are no longer productive and then cast them aside as a bag of trash. Oh yes, trash—for they look like, act like, and feel like trash. Many like Chris came from good homes but fell along the wayside with no place to go. Like the prodigal son, they searched but with a not-so-happy ending. Betsy and I witnessed Chris on a self-destructive path, lonely, and forsaken.

One of the most difficult things we wrestled with during the years before Chris's death was we knew he was so alone. Perhaps it is in some people to be hardhearted, even to their own children, but it was never so with us. At times, during extreme frustration, I felt myself becoming hardhearted, saying things that should not have been said brought heartbreak to his mother. When I said these things, she would be silent, not agreeing nor disagreeing. However, when I saw him, my heart broke because he would look so haggard, tired, and sick.

We struggled with the loneliness of it all. Sometimes, as we would be driving down the road or in downtown Montgomery, a young person would be standing on the street corner or broken down on the Interstate, and we would think about Chris. Thinking about how he was doing today or where he might be. Was he sick? Had he eaten? Some say, "Don't give them money, for you know what drug addicts will do with the money." I know this is true, so we learned never to give large amounts of money. We would pay some bill or some purchase that he might need. We could not get beyond the point of our son so alone in the world, surrounded only by other crack heads or drug dealers. These were the saddest times and the most difficult for us. It is often harder to deal with than death. In death, a family continues on with life, though difficult it may be. Imagine your child walking down the street, outside a restaurant, and asking for money. In my travels around the world, I have been in some restaurant eating and looking out the window, only to see some child or other person standing there and looking at me as I ate. Eating my meal in downtown Panama in one of my favorite restaurants, I noticed a child watching me. Someone who worked at the restaurant went outside to run them away. This bothered me. I could not continue to eat. This child would have liked to have had the scraps that would be thrown away. What a heartbreaking scene.

In Puerto Rico with the United States Air Force one evening, I went out to dinner with some of the men in our group. We enjoyed a good time together laughing and talking and enjoying a good meal. As we departed the restaurant, it had begun to get dark when I was approached by a young lady. She was quite attractive and appeared to be seventeen or eighteen years old. She said to me, "Sir, could you spare some change?" I looked at her, and immediately, my thoughts went to my own son back in Alabama. I did not immediately say anything to her. I just stood there and looked at her, thinking her parents must be worried about her whereabouts. I began to talk with her and ask her what she was doing in Puerto Rico. "Just traveling," she said.

I said, "Do you have family here?"

She said, "No!"

"How did you get here?" The conversation went on, not really going anywhere, for she was not giving many answers.

"Would you go home if I helped you get a ticket home?" No response. I do not know what was happening at home. Perhaps her parents did not have the same feelings we had. Maybe they had kicked her out. Regardless, she was all alone, and I couldn't do anything. I wanted to buy her some food from the local McDonald's. It did not seem that was her interest, so I gave her a little money, knowing she might get drugs. I felt I just had to give her something.

We've all been in this situation at one time or another, not knowing what to do. We want to help, but at the same time, we do not want to help them buy drugs. As we say, "It's a Catch-22." You have to make the best decision you can at that particular time. Perhaps it was because of my son that I gave money to young people.

There was a man standing by himself by his car at the intersection of I-65 and US Highway 31 in the community of Hope Hull, Alabama. I saw him standing there when I pulled in to get gas. It seems people who were down on their luck could always pick me out as a person who could not turn people away. I always thought if I were kind to someone else's child, perhaps that person would be kind to my son. As I pumped my gas, I saw him coming toward me. He was dressed nicely, and his car tag indicated he was from Butler County, Alabama. Coming up to me, he said, "Mister, I do not want to bother you, but I am on my way home and do not have enough gas to get there. I am on my way home to Georgiana, Alabama. If you could help me get a little gas so I can get home, I will give you these tools."

I thought about Chris, who was the world's champion in running out of gas. We had joked in times past if he knew he would make it two miles up the road, he would head out. He had done the same thing this young man was doing and sometimes worse by getting gas and driving off.

"I do not want your tools, son, but if you will pull your car over here, I will put some gas in your car." I put $10 of gasoline in his car and said, "Good luck."

Imagine not having a dime in the world; not even enough to buy yourself a hamburger or pack of crackers. I learned many years ago about what it meant to see someone hungry. I was approached by a young boy on the streets of Bangkok, Thailand. I was only nineteen years old. He had with him his small sister, who looked to be about ten years old. They were hungry and about the dirtiest children I had ever seen. The boy came up to me and attempted to sell his sister to me for $5. I thought to myself, I cannot imagine being that bad off. I learned this was common.

I came from small-town Alabama and had never seen this sort of thing. I was astounded and had not a clue as to what to do. I felt embarrassed seeing this little girl standing there looking at me, and I did nothing. The image has been in my mind over the years. Perhaps this is what has driven me in helping others. The prodigal son from the parable in Luke 15 is typical of so many children who feel they must go into the world and find their way. When they get where they're going, they find it isn't what it's made out to be. From reading the story of the father, there probably would have been a mother sitting at home worrying about their son, wondering what he was doing and where he was, and wishing for him to come home.

This is a parable of a young man who becomes dissatisfied with living at home. Some have called this the parable of the wonderful father. This son goes to his father, asking him for his portion of his inheritance so he could find his own way in life. His father, I am sure, gave it to him reluctantly. The son departed for parts unknown to a life unknown. With money in his pocket, he went to some distant location and begins to party and enjoyed his money along with his friends. At some point he ran out of money. With no money and no place to go, he looked for work. The only thing he could find was feeding the pigs. He went from the top to the bottom, and the bottom was bad. It was as bad as it got. He was now dirty, tired, and hungry and eating the pigs' slop. For the Jews it doesn't get any worse than this. His thoughts returned home to his mother and father. He knew at that point there was nowhere else he could go but home. With that decision made he started home to a reception he never expected and did not deserve.

"The pig pen." Chris was in the pig pen and Mom was there to help clean him up. Just as the father of the prodigal son would stand every day watching for his son's return, so would Betsy,

Chris's mother. She was always waiting for her son to come home. She always welcomed him with open arms.

It's not until a person gets to this point they want to change and do better. In counseling, we were told Chris would need to hit rock bottom before he would want to come back. It's hard to sit at home and wait for that telephone call.

My brother was gone for many years. One day, a Greyhound bus stopped in front of our house, and our long-lost brother, having been gone for so long, walked up to the door. My father was sitting in his chair just inside the door when he saw him. Jumping up, he ran to him and hugged him, welcoming him home as though he had never left. Nothing was said; no questions were asked, like "Where have you been all this time?" It was just a joyous time of a son, a brother, returning home.

The young man in the parable in the Bible was in the gutter and feeling so lonely. The Bible says, "He came to himself," meaning there's got to be something better than this. I have a loving family at home, a father and mother who love me. In his mind, he was thinking what so many others have thought over the years: it's time to go home. He does go home to a joyous reception.

God gave us an example of how he would accept his children home with no questions asked about what they did and how they wasted their life. Should we not accept our children the same way?

Alone, without a dime, how many children are living in the streets of our nation desiring to go home but feeling like they have no place to go? We all see the signs for "Safe Place." It might be a McDonald's or some restaurant or hospital that has opened the doors, allowing young people to come in so they might feel safe and receive help. Our homes should always be a safe place where our children can come home.

No One Cares

Rejection! Have you ever felt rejected, like no one cares, the world is a bad place, and everybody is against you? At one time or another, we all feel this way. Perhaps as a child when we did not receive something we wanted from our parents, we felt rejection.

A drug addict feels rejected and rightly so. People who have mental illness oftentimes feel rejected, even when they are not. It's in their mind that no one cares for them. Their self-esteem is low and they cannot succeed, even though many are highly intelligent. The frustration, brought about by all of this, numbs the mind as we search for answers. Mental illness leads people down roads they don't want to go. They say, "Life is a bummer and everybody hates me." Believe me, I know. I have been in the mind of my son, a manic depressant, who eventually ended it all. Life, as far as he was concerned, was not worth living.

In times past, people who had mental illness or retardation were rejected by society and by their families simply because they did not know what else to do. There were many times we did not know what to do or where to turn. Whenever Chris came to a gathering, all of a sudden, everyone would start whispering. They were saying, "Watch out for that Brady boy." There were times I did not want Chris around.

Rejection is a terrible thing both for the child and family. I could see it in his face when he arrived at a gathering, and he knew everyone was talking about him. No one trusted him, saying, "Why is he here?" To be rejected by society is one thing, but to be rejected by your family brings about even greater heartbreak and destruction of the inner being. He often took his plate of food and went off to sit by himself. At times, I was hard on Chris when he came home. When Chris was treated this way, it always offended Betsy. When we talked, I tried to have her understand why people felt justified in their feelings toward Chris.

I cannot begin to tell you how many times I have seen this when no one, including me, wanted him around. Yet he would show up when there was nowhere else to go. He knew even though we had severe problems with trust, he could come home. The door was never locked to our children when they needed help.

People asked, "Why do you allow him to return home? You know it's going to happen over and over and over again. He will steal your last dollar when he gets the urge for drugs." My reply has always been, and always will be, "When a child cannot come home, where else is there to go?" As already written—but again, for emphasis I say— remember the prodigal son who had been rejected totally by society? He was in the pig pen, alone, with no money and nowhere to go. And he began to think of home.

On every Alabama license plate, "Sweet Home Alabama" is written. I have been in faraway lands, having visited over forty countries, and I cannot even begin to tell you how many times my thoughts returned to home: thoughts of Mom and Dad, and the security of home. After I was married and began to have children, my thoughts would always return to home. Thinking about my children climbing on my lap and just sitting on the front porch and enjoying the day and the solitude that surrounds home makes me think, Yes, there's no place like home. For it is a place of security where even a child who feels rejected should be able to say, "I can go home."

Chris would sometimes call home and say, "Daddy, Mama, I'm out of gas. Could you bring me some?" It always made me mad because it kept on happening, but we never said no. While pouring the gas into his car, I told him, "Chris, this is the last time," with him knowing and me knowing if he called again we would help.

It's not the time to start belittling a child, even an adult child, when bad things happen. They will call because there is no one else. The rejected child will come home because there is nowhere else to go. Some find themselves in the streets doing things that no one would believe them capable of. Turning to prostitution and so many other terrible things, the rejection mounts.

Consider the father of the prodigal son: how often did his thoughts turn to his son, desiring him to return home? I can see this father every day going outside to look up the road to see if there is any sign of his son returning home. Think about this: this son was rejected by society; he had become the worst of the worst. There was nothing lower than the pigpen. Slop was all he had to eat.

Have you ever seen a person like this? You think to yourself, She's a slut, or He's nasty and dirty. And you want your children to stay away from them. People have said these things about our son, and we completely understand their feelings and hold no ill will because we too have felt this way. However, our hearts would come almost to the breaking point, because somewhere out there, our son was lying in a crack house and, as soon as his money was all gone, would be kicked out onto the street once again with no place to go.

Have you ever watched the television show Branded? Listening to the song at the beginning of the show, one hears, "Branded when you know you're a man." I've often thought about how many people who are rejected are really good people, but because of circumstances they put themselves in, they're rejected even though they have good hearts. They're branded a bad person. Chris had a good heart and helped people when they needed help, but he was branded.

There were times in Chris's teen years when his anger could not be controlled and he destroyed things. Later, his anger turned into something else controlled by the drugs he was taking. He then was branded a crack head. Crack heads are rejected by society, by families, and even by churches who do not want them around. The drugs destroy their personalities; it destroys their entire being. They are branded as though with a hot iron, where everyone can see they're a bad person. But just because a person is an addict doesn't always mean they are bad. People just normally reject drug addicts. Rejection is difficult to overcome and oftentimes leads to suicide. One can read a lot of those things into those words, such as "no one wants me around," "nobody trusts me," and "there's nowhere else to go." So many thoughts must enter the mind of an individual before they commit suicide.

My advice to parents who are experiencing these situations is to never turn your back on your children. They are not always pleasant to be around when they're mentally ill or when they have a drug addiction or some other unpleasant problem. I know these are difficult situations for parents to handle. Parenting is on-the-job training, and we as parents are going to make so many mistakes along the way. Some of our mistakes cannot be corrected and will end with bad results. All we can do then is live with our decisions.

His mother was the one person in his life who never rejected him. I admit I rejected my son simply because I did not understand his addiction and mental illness. I suppose the biggest reason was I had no control over the situation. I was the one who was supposed to be calling the shots at home, and he would not listen. However, it seemed his mother was the only one who understood, and he'd never felt rejected by her. Never!

When a person feels this way, it leads them to despair, and despair leads to suicide simply because they feel there is nowhere else to go. Life is not worth living.

Our son killed himself because he felt rejected; he felt so alone, and the world was closing in around him. He went the way of so many before him. My heart says, "When he needed us the most, we were not there." Would it have changed the outcome? Would it have delayed the inevitable? I do not know. I only know rejection has to be the worst form of treatment one could experience.

Our Lord Jesus Christ hung on the cross, having been rejected by all, even by those who were closest to him, like Peter, who cursed and said, "I do not know him," (Matthew 26:74, KJV) or the disciples, when the Bible says 'They all forsook him, leaving him to his enemies," (Matthew 26:56, KJV). Hanging on the cross, totally rejected, he cried out, "My God, my God, why hast thou forsaken me?" (Matthew 27:46, KJV). Jesus was all alone. It does not get worse than that.

People who are rejected feel they have no other recourse left for them and often feel alone, but they have a deep need for someone they know to be with them in hard times.

Chris was to appear before a judge in Jefferson County, having been in the county jail for forty days for a bond hearing. He was brought in with chains on his feet and handcuffs on, looking haggard from a very difficult stay. He looked very depressed and disoriented as he was led into the courtroom. David, Jim, and I were sitting there to encourage him. They had never seen him this way, and it embarrassed Chris. This was the only time he would not look at the observers in the courtroom. This had an effect on me, as I am sure it had on his brothers. The judge then did something I do not remember ever happening before. He asked, "Is there anyone in the courtroom with Chris Brady?" I spoke up, "I am his father, and these are his brothers." We were all asked to come down and stand beside him. This also would be the first time his brothers had appeared in court. I did not know why the judge wanted us down front. This judge looked to me to have compassion about him I had not seen in some of the others. Maybe he had someone close to him who was dealing with some of the same issues. Perhaps he was a Christian and remembering when Jesus stood all alone before judges. Whatever the case, he was kind and considerate to Chris's needs. He knew why Chris was there, for he had all of his records before him and was bound by law as to what he had to do, but he was still kind. Regardless of a person's circumstances, there is never a time one should be mean or unkind to people.

I saw something I had not seen before in my son. This time he was not putting on a show. Chris's need for someone to be with him was seen by this judge, for he really looked bad, and the judge knew he needed someone who loved him next to him. Everyone should have someone to stand beside them in difficult times, even when the difficulties are of their own making. I did not always understand this until I stood beside him in the courtroom. Standing there looking at him on that day, I came to a decision. Wherever Chris was, whatever situation he found himself in, I was going to be there.

Yes, as Chris grew older, there would be many bad times, and as parents, we would make mistakes and even make wrong decisions, but where there is life, there is hope.

LOVE AND HOPE

Betsy and I taught our children from a very young age to always say, "I love you," and mean it. We wanted them to know it is never a shameful thing to express love for each other and be able to hug one another, even in public. This is not something to be ashamed of. People should see it and hear it often.

The Bible talks about how short life is. James tells us life is like a vapor that appears for a short time and vanishes away. James 4:14 (KJV) tells us that life is a delicate thing. One day, all is well, and the next, tragedy strikes. I have known people over the years I should have visited, only to learn they had passed away. Are there things you need to say to your children? Are there things you would like to say to them? Say them! I know people who cannot even talk to their children. Children are children and desire our attention. Without our attention, without our time, they will eventually find someone else who will listen and who will take time when we did not. Children cannot live without the love and tenderness that comes from their parents.

We need to love our children. Everyone would like the perfect child, a child born with all of their faculties, as we would say, normal. As children begin to grow, they experience a world full of problems. People can be so cruel, even to their children who depend upon them. We have all read about unconditional love, and yet, so often, do not practice it. It says, "I will love you, regardless of what you may do or say to me. I will love you, even though you may not be perfect."

We need to understand what God meant about love in 1 Corinthians 13. Love knows no boundaries and no borders, for God so loved each one of us so much that he would even give his only son, his only begotten son (John 3:16, KJV). This simply means God gave the only one of the kind. He taught us about unconditional love. In our story, we want you to know that unconditional love is hard but necessary.

On the day our son took his life, the last words I said to him as I departed at five minutes after four in the afternoon was, "I love you, son." He replied to me, "I love you too, Dad." These are the words I shall never forget. Even in all of the bad times, I never forgot to express to Chris my love for him.

He decided to move back to Missouri to escape the so-called friends he had been keeping company with. He had no money and no car, but he needed to get away, and we knew it. I was totally frustrated and knew something had to give. Perhaps I was wrong. I shall never know, but at the time, I felt this was the right thing to do. I had another car I was not driving very much, so I gave him the car with the stipulation that he had to move, for we could no longer deal with the drugs. I felt like I had abandoned him. I knew Chris would perhaps not even make it to Missouri. Maybe he would stop in Birmingham and obtain drugs with money I was going to give him to help him get started in Missouri. I decided to follow him all the way to Tupelo, Mississippi.

We pulled over beside the road. I said to him as we stood there talking, "Son, I love you more than life itself. I just don't know what else to do." He looked at me and said, "I love you, Dad. Thank you for helping me." I grabbed him, and we hugged each other standing there beside the road. I said to him, "Call me as soon as you get to Missouri." One thing you could always depend upon was that Chris was going to call. He always expressed his love, as all of our children do. Before we hang up the phone, we always say, "I love you."

Betsy showed her love through her actions, not just her words. Chris had been out most of the night, and she had stayed up worrying. I was on a cross-country trip with the air force. Betsy got her coat and car keys and went looking for him. She looked in all the places he had hung out before and drove through bad sections of Montgomery County, where crack houses were known to be. She drove for a long time and then remembered there was a place she had not looked not far from our house. This was a very dangerous area. She drove slowly down the road and looked for his car. Crack addicts often smoke their crack where they buy it. Crack dealers like this because they keep them there until they are broke. As she drove, she saw his car. Backing up, she just pulled up in the yard and demanded they send Chris out. Later, we would actually laugh at what this must have looked like. Imagine a five-foot-two-inch woman pulling up and getting out in front of a crack house and demanding they send her son out. They looked out and said, "Lady, you better get out of here."

She replied, "I know Chris is in there, and you better send him out." She did not have a clue what she would do if they did not. He did come out, and she, by the grace of God, got him back to the house. How old was he then? In his twenties. One might say, "I would have just let him be." We have said that many times, and it's probably true. She should have just let him stay there, but how would she have lived with herself if she had not tried?

The only thing that will carry you through hard times, difficult times, and trying times is love for one another. As we sat in the courtrooms and watching Chris be led in with chains about his ankles and his hands handcuffed before him was heartbreaking. At those difficult times, one has to forget why they're here. I could have sat there and said, "You deserve what you're getting," but I wanted to support Chris and let him know that he was loved. We never supported Chris in the wrong he did, but we were always there, just to let him know how much he was loved.

People often say, "I love my family but I just cannot say it." Some even say, "I was not raised that way." Expressing love, showing love! "It's not that I do not love them, I just cannot say it." "I cannot show outward affection, especially in front of others." Children need to see Mom and Dad kissing and demonstrating love for one another. My oldest son is forty-two years old, and we hug every time we see each other.

How are your children going to learn to love one another or demonstrate love for others? By what they see in their parents. If they have parents who demonstrate love, who express love, usually they will be loving and kind parents. Love your children. Let them not only hear it, but let them see it. I will promise you one thing, if you do not say it and you do not demonstrate, you will regret it.

There are many things I regret, for there were so many things I said in times of frustration. I cannot bring any of them back. I cannot retract anything I have said, but one thing I can truthfully say is I never ceased loving my son and was devastated the day he took his life.

The Bible says, "There is faith, hope, and love, but the greatest is love" (1 Corinthians 13:13, KJV). In all of the terrible times we experienced, we always had hope his life would turn around. In the final analysis, there is always hope. When hope is lost, nothing else really matters.

It doesn't matter what your child has done or how bad they may act, a parent should never give up fighting for their children, even when they get older. Oftentimes, we as parents are their final hope, which even then may not be enough. God gives us a reason to hope.

We all know these words, do we not? We all know how important faith is in our lives. For without faith, it is impossible to please God (Hebrews 11:6, KJV). Pleasing God should be the most important aspect of our lives. And to please God, we must be good parents.

In everything, there is hope. There is always hope, for if you give up hope, there's nothing else left. We loved Chris with all of our ability to love. We demonstrated it when he cursed us and was not very lovable. We became frustrated and said things we should not have said, and after he had gone to bed or left the house, his mom and I would always sit up and talk about tomorrow. I would tell her it was going to get better—one way or the other—it was going to get better. Little did I know at the time what the end would be like. We would sit and cry and hold each other. Many nights, I lay in bed and heard his mother crying silently, for we did not know where he was. We've had opportunities to talk to other parents who were experiencing these same situations. Sometimes they would ask us, "How do you cope with it? It's literally driving us crazy." Sometimes I would ask them if they have a church home. Some did, and some did not. We did learn those who had strong church families were coping better than those who did not. The Bible tells us in Galatians, chapter 6, to bear one another's burdens. I understand that to mean we, as Christians, ought to encourage one another, support, and help one another when times are bad and when times are good. I always said to them, "Never give up hope. Never." If a person gives up, they're going to lose. For as long as there's hope there's a chance to save a life. This is biblical. There's not a day that goes by I do not think about how it might have been had Chris lived.

As long as our son was alive, there was always hope he was going to get better. Sometimes we sat and talked and said, "Chris, when you think about taking drugs, think about those two boys––your sons. Let them be your therapy. Let them be your support system, or your reason not to take drugs." We never at any time thought that one day he would not overcome his addiction.

Bipolar disorder was something else. There is hope because many live with this disease. So often it ends in tragedy, but there's always hope. We never gave up. At no time did we ever say to Chris, "There is no hope for you." However, there were times when we thought there would never be daylight at the end of the tunnel due to all the frustrations.

One can never know the frustrations of dealing with a child who is mentally ill and also has a severe drug addiction unless they have been through it. One cannot say, "I understand what you're going through," unless they've been there. But hope—there is always hope; as long as they are breathing, there is hope. If you or someone you know is struggling with either mental illness or drug addiction, please never give up. I truly believe God said he would not put more upon us than we can bear. Sometimes the load is heavy and we struggle long, but the strength that comes from God is there.

THE LAST COURT
APPEARANCE

One day, about a month before Chris died, he went to court for forging checks. I could give you a long story, as I am sure other parents could to try to justify everything that was done. I could also lash out at the judge, at the police, and others. I never did try to justify the wrongs Chris did, and I will not now.

We arrived at the courthouse with Chris. This was the day Chris was to be sentenced for the crime of forging checks. Everything had been prearranged by his court-appointed lawyer. He would get to serve his time in what was called "drug court." At least, that is what we understood. Maybe we just did not understand what the lawyer had said. Drug court is where those who had drug offenses could, under the oversight of the court in a very strenuous way, help an individual overcome the drug addiction and become good citizens and a productive person in society. There were some very strenuous rules one must follow in order to be qualified for this particular program. We were told Chris was qualified, that the judge was going to allow him drug court; therefore, we were all very upbeat about the fact that maybe this was where Chris was going to get his new lease on life, his new start. He knew if he did not finish drug court, he would go to prison for the crime and must, at that time, serve out all of his time. We were all standing nervously outside the courtroom. Chris could not stand still because he was so nervous. These cases were already worked out ahead of time in negotiations with the judge, lawyer, and the defendant. Chris's case was the last one for the day. We were sitting there waiting, having not yet seen his lawyer because she was late. The judge asked us why we were there, and at that time, she walked into the courtroom. Chris's name was called, and the crimes he was being charged with were read before the court so all could be recorded. We were sitting in the back of the courtroom, with Chris standing before the judge, looking up at him. His lawyer was standing to his right. Remember, he had already been promised, or so we understood, he would get drug court. His lawyer did say he would probably have to spend the night in jail. Chris said that was no problem; he would be getting out on the next day and could deal with the one night in jail.

Chris knew he was facing some very serious charges before him and was ready to pay the price, but none of us knew what that price was going to be.

As the charges, twenty-six counts of forged instruments in the first degree, were read against Chris, we sat and waited and even wondered how it came to all of this. Even today, I wonder why. I suppose all parents always wonder why. Where did I go wrong as a parent? These things were going through my mind as we sat there and waited for the judge to begin.

"Mr. Brady, do you understand the charges that have been read here today?" "Yes, sir," Chris replied.

"You have pled guilty to twenty-six counts of possessing a forged instrument. Do you understand I can give you ten years on each count?"

"Yes, sir," Chris replied.

"According to the laws of the state of Alabama, I now sentence you to a term of ten years on each count."

Betsy looked at me, and I looked at Betsy. She started to cry, and his girlfriend was crying. I was unable to even make a move. We were all dumbfounded. He had done a lot of things but had never been convicted in a court of law for anything other than stealing my chainsaw. He turned around and looked back at us. His eyes told the story, for then he knew he was going to the penitentiary for a long time. Two hundred and sixty years; of course, he would not have to serve 260 years because they had already worked how much time he would serve. I thought to myself, He is only guilty of writing checks. Murderers don't get this many years. At that moment, we were unaware about the deal that had been worked out by the court. Then it became reality when the deputy came up behind Chris and put handcuffs on him.

Of all that had happened, this was the hardest on his mother. I had been there when handcuffs had been put on, but his mom had never seen him in handcuffs, and it was traumatic. Court was over. We stood up while the judge left the room. We were unable to speak to Chris as they led him away. He glanced back one last time as he departed the courtroom.

The lawyer said to the judge, "Your Honor, tomorrow is the birthday of his son. Could he be released until then?"

The judge simply said, "He should have thought about that earlier."

Don't get me wrong. I'm not questioning the judge or the court system; however, I don't believe it makes any arrangements for those who are simply drug users. There is an effort, and one is drug court, but so few are helped here. I wish I had the answer, but I do not. As a father who has watched his son destroy himself, I believe there is a different method, a different way, in helping the drug user, and prison is not the place for them.

What is the answer? I wish I could find one. The following is my opinion, perhaps written in frustration. The system is broken and needs to be repaired. The large part of the population of our prisons is there because of drug-related crime. I would be the first to say that I do not have the answer. I wish I did. We as a nation and as a people need to wake up. Our leaders and our judges who must enforce the laws must find a way to control the trafficking in drugs. The police catch a person with a rock of crack cocaine, and now this person must face a judge. Our son was where he was because of drugs. Let's spend more money on educating against the use of drugs. We must win this battle before it is too late. The scene we witnessed in that courtroom is a scene all over America. Families sit and watch as their loved one is sentenced and their hands are tied. There now is nothing else to do but visit them in prison.

We walked outside the courtroom and stood there, just trying to make sense out of all of it. Was there any sense? Was there any justice? Our hearts were broken, and the sad thing about it was we could not do anything. The lawyer came out of the courtroom and said that Chris would be released in a couple of days to enable him to make a court appearance in Birmingham, which stemmed from another bout with the law. He would be told when to report to the department of corrections to start serving his sentence. We found out at this time he would in all probability have to serve three years in prison.

The end was nearing. He said everything was closing in on him and there was nowhere to go. He also knew how important it was not to run, for had he ran, we could lose our house. He had assured his mother, "Don't worry about your house. I'm not going anywhere." He did not try to leave the state but rather went to Birmingham as instructed to stand before another judge. Where else was there to go? He was definitely going to prison. That was a fact. He had no money and no job, and the relationship he was in was going downhill.

Sitting on the porch following his sentencing and waiting for instructions on when he was to report, I said to him, "Son, you can do three years standing on your head. Your mom and I will be there. We will make sure the children do not forget you."

He said to me, "Dad, I'm really not overly concerned about going to prison. If it had been for a long time, I don't know how I could handle that. I just want to know my children will be okay. I want you to know how much I love you and Mom. Another thing, Dad, I'm sorry for all I put you and Mom through."

For some reason or another, suicide never crossed my mind, for he talked so sensibly and so seriously and with such great remorse. I remember feeling this could be the turning point in his life. Yes, he and I had words not less than twenty-four hours before, and now we were having this conversation. This was on Saturday, less than twenty-four hours before his death. Had I only known this would be our last conversation. There were so many things I wish I had said.

Was it drugs that caused Chris to take the course of action he took? No. It was his mental condition. Drugs, sex, and the inability to cope with life are the results of mental illness. It was not drugs that pushed him over the top. I talked with him shortly before he stepped off the steps and took his life. He was in a very bad relationship with a girl who would feed him pills. Pills she was taking for her own problems. She said, "It helps him." We tried to tell him she was bad for him, but this was to no avail. He had no security, no money, and a drug problem, and all of a sudden, it all closed in on him, and it was more than he could take.

THE END IS HERE

On Friday before Chris died, Chris asked me to go with him in my truck to get some pine straw he had promised to spread. We had words over the fact he always promised that which he could not deliver. He would do this many times, and then someone would have to go with him to obtain the supplies to complete the project. I did go with him on this day, but reluctantly.

I worked all day with him, laying pine straw. As the day progressed, we actually had a good time, laughing and joking about different things and places we had been. It turned out to be a fun day.

Sunday morning began with us preparing to go to church. It was a normal day. Betsy and I had our coffee and talked. Chris came in, and we had a confrontation. He was upset, I was upset, and Betsy was upset. I told him that the continued situation he always found himself in must stop somewhere. He got upset. "What do you want me to do, Chris?" I replied. "Your mother and I have given and given until there is nothing left to give.

We will move out, and you can have the house, but things have to change."

"Every time you two get in the same room, you argue," Betsy said. We did not always argue, but we did a lot, and that never helped the situation, but I had had it. I think every parent reaches a point where they know something must give. It seems we had tried everything possible. We were at a turning point, and it seemed there was nothing else we could do for him, for he continued to use drugs and spend all his money on them. The next day, he would need money for gas or cigarettes. "Chris," I would say, "I don't even smoke, and you want me to buy you cigarettes." I usually purchased him cigarettes just to have peace.

Betsy and I left for church that morning and were to have lunch with a family from church, not knowing this was the last day in the life of our son. If we had only known, we thought. How many have reasoned that way? If I had only known, I would not have said what I did, or I would have done something different. "If" is such a big word. How many have said "if?" We departed for church while Chris stayed home with his girlfriend, who was visiting from Cullman, Alabama. They were also having problems and argued with each other throughout the day.

We returned from church around two p.m. There was a confrontation between him and me, which upset Betsy to the point that she took our grandchildren and went to Montgomery to the home of one our sons.

Around four, I got ready to go to church. That day, I was to make a Panama Missions presentation at a church in Pike County, Alabama. Before I left, Chris came out to the truck and asked me if I could help him get his license from Tennessee over the Internet. He had lost his license due to non-payment of a traffic ticket. I told him I would but needed to hurry so I would not be late. We were not successful in getting the license, and I asked him,

"Why not just go to Tennessee and get the license?" He told me he would have to go all the way to Palaski, Tennessee. He had lost his license so many times that I was really tired of helping him get it back, but he needed them to keep his job.

I told him goodbye and that I loved him, and he responded that he loved me too. Little did I realize that this would be the last time I would say, "I love you" to my son.

I then left, departing the house at five minutes after four. After I left, Chris evidently became extremely frustrated, for reasons I am not aware of, and went out to the utility room and found an electrical cord and brought it back to the house. He took the cord and tied it on the beam of the porch and put it around his neck. He told his girlfriend he was too tall and needed to find another place. She did not take him seriously, even when he put the cord around his neck. She later said, "I just didn't think he would do it." He then went inside the house and, for some reason, pulled his clothes off, and threw the cord around the beam closest to the steps, and then he jumped off the steps and hung himself from the rafters of our Pintlala home, bringing an end to the misery he felt in his life. Summed up in his own words, "I cannot handle life anymore."

I have often wondered if I had stayed home how it might have affected the outcome. He seemed okay and did not look like someone who was contemplating suicide. Was he, at that moment, contemplating suicide? I do not think so, and neither did the investigators. At that moment, I do not believe he was thinking about taking his life. He was somewhat agitated. He surely did not act like someone who would be dead in an hour. I do not know what transpired during that last hour between him and his girlfriend. Did they argue? Their relationship was in trouble. Small things in the mind of the mentally ill can very rapidly become big things. They believe there is no answer.

According to Chris's girlfriend, the telephone would not work because he had ripped it from the wall. She ran to my brother's house and called Betsy rather than 911. Betsy was in Montgomery, seventeen miles away, and had two of our grandchildren in the car. The call was frantic, saying, "Chris is hanging himself." These were the words she used. "Is hanging." Betsy, thinking she was at the house with Chris, told her to get Chris and push up on him. Betsy and Chris's wife had saved his life before using this method. She told Betsy she was at my brother's house. Betsy said, "Call 911. I am on my way." The call to 911 was made. The girlfriend said, "I need to get back to the house," but was told by the 911 operator not to return, for it had been too long. She had to wait for the emergency vehicles.

I am thankful they arrived before Betsy. Betsy drove in excess of one hundred miles an hour to try to save Chris. She had done it before, why not now? I do not believe it ever occurred to her she could not save him. It was not to be. Chris was dead long before she arrived.

She screamed his name over and over and over, lying in the front yard, saying, "Just let me touch him, please let me touch him." She was finally moved into my brother's house and then transported by ambulance to the hospital because of heart and blood pressure problems.

I arrived around seven fifteen, having received a call from one of my sisters. Her words were, "Larry, its Chris."

I knew at that very moment and asked her the question, "Is he dead?"

Her reply was, "Yes. You need to get home. Betsy needs you." She told me Betsy had collapsed. I drove as fast as I could and was met in my front yard by a deputy who made me get back in the truck until I calmed down. When I first saw Betsy, I was heartbroken because she was hurting so badly. I had never seen her that way. It seems the last time I saw her cry so much was when Chris ran away and we could not find him for several days. I could do nothing to control her tears or comfort her. Betsy and I cried together. We were crushed.

At one point in his life, when nothing seemed to be going right, he said to me, "Life is just not worth living."

My reply was, "Chris, just look around you. There is so much to be thankful for. Your mom and I love you. We just hate what you are doing to yourself and the rest of the family."

How many people have felt just this way and come on the verge of or committed suicide? I know people say, "This is the easy way out." He didn't stay around and work it out or try to get the right kind of help. He just took the easy way.

Before Chris killed himself, he wrote two letters: one to his mom and the other to his girlfriend. One can only read the letter to his girlfriend and know they were having a hard time in their relationship. The letter simply stated:

> Baby, my mind is tired. I love you with all my heart. I hope you will always remember me. I never meant for any of this to happen. I hope you find happiness. I can't go on living this way. I'm sorry for all the pain. I hope you will always keep me in your heart. Take care of yourself. Love, Chris

It would be several weeks before we were able to read the letter Chris had left because of an on going investigation by the sheriff's department. These are the words no family wants to hear, a letter no one wants to find. No one can describe the feeling when it happens.

A family never gets over the death of a child; we just learned to live with it. I read where some fathers get over the death of a child in two years or less. At times, when I think about Chris, it puts me into a very depressed mood, and writing about this has helped me deal with what has happened.

In all of our tears and our shouts of anguish, the hurt just would not get better. This was a horrible day forever embedded in our minds. There was nothing anyone could say, no words––absolutely nothing. We truly loved the people who came and just wanted to hug and to give comfort. We felt no comfort, for our world had collapsed around us.

Betsy later commented through her tears, "Death is so final." We cannot bring the dead back. We can only mourn and try to get through the next days. I read a poem one time that said, "The clock of life is wound but once and where it stops no one knows."

When the clock of life does stop, we are never prepared for it. Every one of us has been to funerals to try to comfort the grieving, to try to say the right thing, and wanting to do what you can to help a person feel just a little bit better.

Someone said to me about two weeks after Chris died, "Your son is not the first, and he won't be the last. Others have faced this tragedy, and many will face it again." So true, but it did little to make us feel better. We also get back to the very fact of how final death is. The Bible says in Acts 17:30, "First comes death and after this judgment" (KJV). The old are going to die. The young may die. We just don't know when. This passage speaks of death that proceeds judgment; it's something no one can escape, but no one expects it to come this way. On this day, friends and neighbors from the community arrived. There must have been fifty people in our yard, everyone wanting to help, to be able to say just the right thing, but what does one say in a situation like this? The family gathered around. Everyone was trying to comfort each other. We were all concerned about Betsy. There was no comfort. Just the screams of a mother who felt she had failed. The cries of the father who also felt he had let his son down. As a father, I tried to answer questions—the questions of law enforcement, questions from the rescue squad, and so many wanting to know what they could do to help; however, there is nothing that can be done now. Things would never be the same again for a part of me and Betsy died on this day. As a parent, what does one say? What makes things better and eases the pain children feel? As parents, we want to help, to comfort, to provide what is needed, but sometimes, all we can do is be there.

Betsy was unable to comfort and needed to be comforted. What could we do? What could we say? There were no words and there was no comfort; we only had the image of our son as he hung from our rafters.

I remember thinking, Maybe I will wake up in a few minutes, and it will all be over. I remember thinking, He will come back. There is that time of denial. This is not happening; it's just a dream, a bad dream. You see, Chris always came back, but not this time. That day, we were not dreaming. Mike and I took down the beam he used to remove the marks the cord left, but the mark in our mind can never be removed. No manner of talking or counseling can remove it. This only helps one deal with a tragedy. Life goes on.

There are a lot of questions that needed to be answered. The sheriff's department had to investigate, and the coroner showed up to take charge. Chris was dead! Reality had not yet set in. I had never felt so useless. I was dazed, and I looked into our house where his body was. People were talking to me, but I did not hear. They wanted to know what they could do. Even now, I often come home and sit and look at the spot where he died, thinking back on the good times we had. There were many good times.

Betsy and I often will go out on the back corner of the porch where Chris spent a lot of time. It was his favorite spot. I fussed about the cigarette butts on the ground and would say, "Chris, when I was in the military, I refused to pick up other peoples' cigarette butts if I did not smoke them. Now get out there, and pick them up." He would look at me and grin and say, "Ah, Pop, calm down. I'll pick 'em up." I would make coffee, and he would say, "You mean we got to drink your wimpy coffee?"

Each person writes his or her own book while living upon this earth. Once written, it cannot be changed. Would it not be great if we could hit an "undo" button like we do on a computer and all the bad things we have done in life would be gone? We could then start a new sentence and another chapter. However, this is not real life. Life is not like a movie, where the scene will be recorded over and over until the director gets it the way he wants it. If the scene is not right, the editors will go back and take out the bloopers. Life is full of bloopers one cannot remove. We can only learn from these bloopers and mistakes, even when they have a tragic ending. Chris's book was written, and it did not have a happy ending.

On September 18, 2005, the day Chris hung himself from the rafters in our home, the book Chris was writing ended.

Four years later, that day is still fresh on my mind as though yesterday. You might say September is a month to be remembered around the Brady house. On the second day of September 1999, Chris's first son came into the world. On the fourteenth day of September 1977, Chris was born. On the eighteenth day of September 2005, Chris died. On September 22, he was buried. September 28, 1954, Betsy was born. And on September 30, 1978, Michael was born. Yes, there's much in September, and while there are some great things to celebrate—the birthday of a grandchild, the birthday of a mother, and of another son—the one thing that puts a dark side to this month is the day our son died.

RETURNING HOME

After Chris passed away, people arrived to express their condolences, bringing food and trying to help out any way they could. Our next-door neighbor arrived, bringing food, and stood there in our living room and cried. Many people came, and stories were told about what they remembered, with everyone trying to put a brighter side on a very bad situation. Isn't this what friends and church families are about? The Bible tells us in Galatians 6:1–2 (KJV), "Bear ye one another's burdens." There is no greater burden to bear, it would seem, than what we were going through. Later, someone would ask how we were able to come back to the very house where Chris had killed himself. We had to go back and soon. Returning to the house the following day, the following morning, was not easy, but we knew we had to go home, or we might not return at all.

We turned into our driveway and sat there for a period of time. As we looked down our driveway, we could see the beauty of it all. My brother Buddy had worked many hours and days after he retired to make things look so beautiful. Each one of us worked to make our part of the homeplace beautiful. Turning into our driveway off of US Highway 31, the house where I was raised is on a hill to the left. My brother received the house from my mother after the death of my father because he loved it so much. A cousin who attended one of our family reunions said, "This place looks like a park." And it does; it's beautiful. Traveling down the driveway, one will pass our family cemetery on the right. Chris is buried there. Passing by the cemetery, our driveway turns to the right, and my brother's driveway continues on. The three brothers live on the old homeplace where we all grew up and where we shall all be buried.

Our house sits nestled in to the edge of the forest. All of our children love coming home, for we have made this a place to enjoy and a place for our grandchildren and others to come. Chris loved this place and always enjoyed sitting on our back porch, even on cold days. How many conversations, how much laughter, how many tears all happened on that porch?

Our grandchildren have named our house the "brown house." It is named this because it looks brown with the wood siding we used when we built the house. We wanted our house not to be a showplace, but a place where we as a family can live, play, and not have to worry so much about small things, such as knocking something off the table or breaking some expensive item. Home should always be a place of refuge and a place where the family can share with each other. I never was a fancy person. I suppose I got this from my father, who was a simple man, never owning a car nor having indoor bathroom facilities. He was just a simple man who loved simple things.

My sister June lives across the road where we were all born. Our house burned when I was six years old. We moved across the road, which had been our sweet potato field when I was growing up. My twin sisters, Sharon and Sandra, live with their families just down the road. My sister Betty lives a few miles to the west while my sisters Pat and Diane live on the Brady Road, located to the south just a few miles. Not far from them, my oldest sister, Daisy Ann, lives. Another sister, Verba Lee, is married to a minister and lives outside of Jacksonville, Alabama. There are eleven children, and we all enjoy coming back home. It is there Betsy and I returned to mourn the loss of our son. It is there where he was buried.

While it is always so easy to remember bad things people do, it is the good times we like to remember. On the day we returned home, we made some coffee and went out on the porch to sit, talk, and plan. We sat there for a period of time sipping our coffee. I would lose it and start crying uncontrollably, and Betsy would put her arms around me to comfort me. It hurt so badly, and the pain went so deep. We talked about the night before and discussed all that had occurred over the past several months. We sat there for a while not saying anything, for it seemed there was just not anything else to say. We knew we should get up and go in the house and prepare for people, neighbors, church family, and our own children, who would be arriving soon. However, we did not have the energy and found great solace sitting on the porch looking at some of the flowerbeds Chris had made. We plant the same kind of flowers each year, for Chris loved the many colors. It seemed he was an artist when it came to landscaping. We finally got up, not feeling hungry, so we took our showers and prepared. There was nothing else to do and nothing else to say. People began to arrive as we had expected. Living in this wonderful community where I had been born and spent the better part of my life has been a wonderful place and still is. The Pintlala community has always been very close, demonstrating caring concern for others who are experiencing problems in their lives. People do not realize how important it is to the healing and comfort for those who are hurting. Our community has been part of our lives for generations. My father, his parents, and their parents have all lived here. My father went to the Pintlala School, as all of us did. We are proud of our community and for what we mean to one another. People of different faiths have come together to comfort, to support, and to encourage.

Today was no exception as people began to arrive. As in all situations, people like to talk and to remember family and friends. Some talked about the Brady's growing up. They talked about remembering my dad raising such beautiful gardens with so many vegetables. My dad literally fed the community and enjoyed every moment. He liked giving things away. Yes, people remembered these things, and so we talked about them. None would ask us about how Chris took his life, and we were glad. Oftentimes, people will tell the story over and over again, but not on this day; people were content in giving comfort in a difficult time.

An investigator from the sheriff's department returned to ask some questions that needed to be asked. As in all suicides, an investigation had to be conducted. It wasn't pleasant, but it had to be done. We understood this and dealt with it on this day, answering the questions we were asked.

People often remember things they want to talk about, and later, my sister would write a poem about Chris. My sister Betty had a close relationship with him, remembering when he would come to her house to visit. Through all of his problems and difficulties and addictions, she always had a special relationship with Chris. After his death, she wrote the following poem:

Chris
A handsome young man
With a ready smile upon his face.
Behind the smile of torture,
No one could erase.

When he was just Chris,
Nothing troubling his mind,
The love you could not miss.
He was humble, sweet, and kind.

Two very loving parents,
Who were my best friends,
went with him through problems
until the very end.

Daddy to two little boys,
Special in every way.
The love he had for them, for they were his joy,
Will be reflected in the things they do and say.

When sorrow comes,
And the tears start to flow,
God will send a band of angels
To surround and comfort

The very depths of your soul.
There is no torture now,
No demons and no more pain,
'Till you see him again.

—Sarah Elizabeth Simmons

MAKING FUNERAL
ARRANGEMENTS

After one dies, life continues on, and we had to do what so many have done before—make funeral arrangements. In the case of sudden death, few things had been done to prepare for that moment and for that day. All of us got together in the living room of our house to discuss funeral arrangements. This was an emotional time and required a lot patience and understanding. The big question was, "How are we going to pay for the funeral?" Chris had no insurance. Funerals are not cheap, and even a small funeral costs over $7,000. With no insurance, his brothers pitched in to pay for the funeral.

We moved on to the cemetery to pick out a plot, deciding on one in the corner with enough room for the members of the family when their time came. As we gathered at the cemetery, our thought turned to the moment at hand. One of his brothers commented, "I can't believe he's gone. We did not see eye to eye, and I did not like what he was doing to the family. I am sorry I did not do more to help ease his pain." Each one of his brothers felt deeply about this. They talked about what more they could have done. For now, all we could do was talk and wish we had done more.

We returned to the house to write the obituary for the local newspaper. How many times have we picked up the newspaper to read the obituaries? Nearly everyone I know reads the obituaries. We wrote Chris's obituary that appeared in the Montgomery Advertiser on September 20, 2005:

> Christopher Michael Brady, 29, a resident of Hope Hull, Alabama, died Sunday, September 18, 2005, at his residence. Funeral services will be held on Wednesday, September 21, 2005, at 2:00 p.m. from Leak Memory Chapel with ministers Jack Cates, Clarence Denney, and Clyde Ray officiating. Burial will follow at the Brady cemetery, Pintlala, Alabama. Visitation will be from 5:30 to 8:00 p.m. Tuesday at the funeral home. Survivors include his two sons; parents, Larry and Betsy Brady; brothers, David Brady (Jennifer) of Birmingham, Alabama; Jim Brady (Yvette) of Montgomery, Alabama; Michael Brady (Kim) of Ramer, Alabama; Ricky Brady (Melissa) of Montgomery, Alabama, and nieces and nephews. He was preceded in death by his grandparents, Lewis and Thelma Brady and Homer and Hazel Beck. Memorial contributions may be made to Panama Missions, P.O. Box 451, Hope Hull, AL 36043.
>
> —Montgomery Advertiser

Our appointment with the funeral home was at ten a.m. on September 19. We got up on that morning and went through our normal routine of getting dressed, knowing today, we must discuss the final funeral arrangements.

Jack Cates, minister of the Davenport Church of Christ, was asked to speak at the funeral. Also contacted were a close friend and minister, Clarence Denney, and my brother-in-law, Clyde Ray, minister for the Weaver Church of Christ, to speak. Then there came the task of selecting pallbearers. We asked his cousins and some very close friends to participate.

There were so many details that had to be attended to, and we were in no frame of mind to even think about what needed to be done. We finally left it up to our sons; however, we did travel to the funeral home with them and met with the funeral home director. Financial arrangements were made, and we discussed all the details of the funeral and how we wanted it to be done. A casket was picked out. We found ourselves growing more emotional as the day went on. At this point, we were physically and emotionally exhausted, and it was only the beginning.

There was no mention of our past problems. It was time for a family to come together as one and support one another. We did not talk about who was to blame. We cried buckets of tears and looked at pictures of Chris when he was just a small boy. We wondered when this dream would finally end and we'd wake up. He'd be standing there saying, "Ah, Pop, this coffee you make is for wimps." I thought, "God, if I just had one more chance." There would be no more chances; there would be no more opportunity. We could only sit there and grieve.

Our sons, in planning for the funeral, tried to make the stress of it all as little as possible for us. Sitting around a long table, they talked about what Chris would've liked. He never wore a coat and tie, so he would not wear one on this day but rather some of his favorite clothes—his favorite cowboy shirt, blue jeans with his belt that had the big buckle, and his cowboy boots. This was Chris.

September 20 arrived, the day of visitation at the funeral home. We were to be at the funeral home at five o'clock for the family viewing.

I looked at Betsy as we departed for the funeral home, for she was so exhausted, having so little sleep over the past several days. We arrived at the funeral home and were met by our four sons, their wives, and children. The next hour was very emotional, our private time to be with Chris. We looked down at him lying there so peacefully as though he were asleep. It was hard to believe that the past Friday, he and I were riding together in my truck, going to get some pine straw to put out on a job he had. It was hard to believe that past Sunday afternoon, I said to him one last time, "I love you," and to hear him say to me, "I love you too, Dad." We as family were all gathered around the casket. We didn't remember or talk about the difficulties he experienced in his life. There were no drug problems, no burned lips from smoking crack, and there was no look of despair so often seen on his face. No one discussed the bad times, for it was a time to reflect on our lives and on his life.

People began to arrive by the hundreds to express their condolences. I can never emphasize how important it is to have friends and, more especially, a strong church family. Where would we be in these times without our faith, without our brothers and sisters in Christ, who were there to let us know they loved us?

We departed the funeral home and returned to our home after an exhausting day. No other thought entered our minds. We were consumed with the events we were surrounded with. The day arrived, and we went through the motions of getting ready. Friends and neighbors arrived, bringing food. Some from church came to stay at the house to prepare for all those who would come after the funeral. They lovingly prepared and cleaned, getting ready for the expected crowd after the funeral.

So much food means so many friends and good neighbors living in a wonderful community.

Betsy and I got up early in the morning on September 21 and decided to walk up to the cemetery, where a fresh grave had just been dug. I do not know why we decided to go, but we felt we just wanted to go and meditate and be alone for a few moments. As said before, our cemetery is such a beautiful place, so serene, and people feel they can sit and think about the past, remembering the good times of the loved ones gone before. I suppose this was no different on this day as we decided to take a short walk, for it was a beautiful morning. The sun was shining, and one would not think this was a dark day in the life of our family. As we walked, we looked over at the apple trees, where Chris so much enjoyed eating the apples, and to my brother's garden, which was so beautiful at this time of year. We looked at the pond nearby, where Chris enjoyed fishing, even catching one of the largest bass ever caught out of that pond. We sat down next to the grave on the ground, saying little but thinking much. There was little else to say. There was no need to rehash his life; for now, all we could do was mourn. All we could do was remember the past and pray for the soul of our son. Betsy said, "If I just knew Chris was in heaven, I think I could handle it better." Perhaps my next words were the words or thoughts of so many parents who loved God and thought so much of their eternal destiny. "God is a just God. He knows Chris's heart. He will not make a mistake in the eternal destiny of one who was so troubled, one whose mind was controlled by something so uncontrollable. I know God knows Chris's heart." Those words are true, and I believe true to Scripture. After reading what Chris wrote while in jail, I believe Chris had made his peace with God.

So often, I have heard people pass judgment on someone who has committed suicide, saying they sealed their eternal destiny.

Many believe if a person commits suicide, then they have committed an unpardonable sin. One must repent of the sin before they can be saved. I do not take this position and never have. A person must be in their right mind in order to repent. They must know what they have done is a sin. I fail to believe a person who commits suicide is in their right mind. They are not thinking correctly. If someone believes differently, I respect his or her opinion. God is just and loving and will do the right thing. I believe people like Chris are not thinking correctly.

Betsy and I were sitting where our son would be placed very soon, thinking. Our thoughts were going back to the day we brought him home from the hospital and felt those joyful moments. But this day, he would be laid to rest. Betsy said, "At least he is at peace."

Sitting by the grave, we heard a car approaching. It stopped, and we heard the door close and footsteps of someone approaching. We looked up, and there was one of the sweetest people God ever put on this earth. She now has gone on to heaven to her reward, but on this day, she was thinking of us. She walked up and said, "Can I sit with you all?" I said to her, "Please do," and she sat down next to us on the ground. For a while, nothing was said. We were all in our thoughts, and then she told us how much she loved us. She expressed how she felt for our children and us. We talked about when I was a child attending the Liberty Church. They were tremendous supporters and encouragers of my family and me for many years. Her visit meant so much to us in such a sad time. I expressed this to her son at her funeral.

Betsy and I remained for a little longer and then returned to the house to prepare to go to the funeral home. We arrived early so people could view the body who did not have an opportunity the night before. Then it was time. The funeral director came in and asked all the friends to go into the chapel. We as a family gathered one last time to have a private time with Chris. Our hearts were broken; part of us had died. Standing there, looking down one last time at the body of our son, remembering the words of his note, "Do not forget me." Do not forget me. How can anyone forget one of their children?

The ministers surrounded us while one of them led us in a prayer before we went into the chapel. We were then led into the chapel while Chris's casket was placed before the podium. My good friend and minister friend, Byron Benson, and four other special friends sang three songs: "God's Family," "Amazing Grace," and "Precious Memories." The ministers spoke words of encouragement. Words that touched my heart, for these men were such a part of our family. They knew of Chris's struggles and how it affected us as parents and the effect it had upon his brothers. Everyone moved from the chapel to the many cars lined up for the seventeen-mile drive to our family cemetery in Pintlala. The funeral procession was long, and it took about forty-five minutes to make the drive. As we turned off the main highway, I was amazed at how many cars were in the funeral possession. It took a little while for everyone to gather inside the cemetery, where my brother-in-law, Clyde Ray, spoke of the tragedy of having to bury children.

It seemed we were in a trance. We sat there looking at the casket sitting over an open grave. Each one of us was engrossed in our own thoughts. There were rivers of tears flowing, and there was no comfort—only a sense of deep loss and a realization that Chris was not coming home ever again. We would never have to sit up at night and wait. Forgotten were the frustrations and the turmoil of past years. The frustrations were replaced by grief that seemed almost unbearable.

We were reminded of the memories, some good and some bad, but in that moment, we only thought about the good. A prayer was offered, and the funeral service was over. The ministers came to offer their condolences. We all stood to leave, and Betsy leaned over and placed her hands on the casket for one last time. Time seemed to stand still, for this time there was no coming to the rescue. "Life is like a vapor," says James in the Bible. How many times I have used this passage of scripture at funerals? We stood there looking, thinking, and crying, each within private thoughts. His four brothers helped their mother as she departed the gravesite. There was nothing else to say, for it was all summed up in the suicide note: "Life is not worth living." We could only lament, "Oh, God. Why?"

THE CEMETERY

I suppose most people think of cemeteries as being morbid, dark, dreary places. They can be, if that is how we think of them, but the Brady cemetery we would like to think is different. It is a special place because we have family there. Our son Chris is buried there on the Brady homeplace.

Close to the cemetery is a very large oak tree, and just in front of the tree, my brother built a swing. Sometimes on Thursday nights, my brothers and sisters will gather just outside the cemetery and sit under this oak tree. We come here because of the serenity and beauty. It was here we were all born and raised. We sit here and talk about how it was, often remembering those we love that are buried here.

My sister-in-law—the wife of my older brother—and her infant baby were the first to be buried here, followed by my grandmother, and now there are uncles and aunts, and my brother is buried next to his wife and baby. My mother and father are also buried here. I commented to someone, "There are too many young people in our cemetery." There's also a nephew—who, like my son, committed suicide—and his brother in a freak accident slipped and fell breaking his neck buried next to him. My son is buried in one corner in a very serene spot. The most recent is my niece, who died of leukemia at forty-two years old. Other family members are buried here. It is here we come to visit our son on a regular basis. Every Christmas, we put a Christmas tree next to his grave, for Christmas was his favorite time of the year.

My father loved the homeplace where he too grew up. He wanted to be buried there, not in some distant cemetery. He wanted to stay on the homeplace. He had a plan in his mind as to how he wanted the cemetery. We have since enlarged it and put a fence around with beautiful wrought-iron gates that lead into the cemetery. The gates and columns were designed and built by my brother Allen. To the left of the gate on a plaque are the words from a poem someone once wrote:

> Do not grieve for my going.
> I would not have you sad for a day.
>
> But in summer just gather some flowers,
> And remember the place where I lay.
>
> And come in the shade of the evening,
> When the sun paints the sky in the west.
>
> Stand for a few minutes beside me,
> And remember only my best.
> Anonymous

My sister purchased a statue of an angel and had it placed in the middle as though it were guarding those who rest there. The Brady cemetery is somewhat different than others in that it is located in the middle of our homeplace. One does not need to go to some distant back road or travel to some other community to visit a loved one. We visit often those who rest here. Chris had many friends, some who thought a lot of him. We have noticed, on special days, a flower arrangement left on his grave. It still remains a mystery as to who this person is.

When his children are at the "brown house," they will come to their grammy and say, "Grammy, we are going to see Daddy." They will walk up to the cemetery and look at his grave and his picture. I don't know everything his older son says to his dad, but we have heard him talking to him about a ballgame he had played or his day at school. One day, not long after Chris died, his son, six years old at the time, came to his grammy and said, "Grammy, I didn't get to see my daddy before he went to heaven, and so now I go outside into the sunshine and talk to him."

Yes, our cemetery has been made to be a special place of solitude, and meditation. It has been made a place where people can come and reflect and to reminisce. It is a special place, and we take great pride in making it not just a place for the dead. It is a place for the living to always be reminded of those we love so dearly. As we sit here from time to time, we all reflect on how special and fragile life is.

My sisters change out the flowers for the different times and seasons of the year. There is a big pine tree that shades the cemetery with apple trees nearby, and we all come to pick the apples and enjoy the beauty of the homeplace. Our entire family— composed of brothers and sisters, nieces and nephews, sons and daughters—return to the old homeplace two times a year for a great gathering. On the Fourth of July, we all return for a family reunion, and what a time it is. Each year it seems there is another marker in the family cemetery. We remember those who have died each year.

We sit there at the Brady cemetery often, just outside the gates under the big oak tree, and we talk about the times when we played as children. My mother wrote a poem about the big oak tree. It was in this tree we played as children, and under this tree, some received their first kiss. It is a tree with so many memories. This tree is now gone, but the memories continue to flood our souls. My mother wrote the following poem about this tree.

I dropped an acorn on the ground,
It took root in fertile sod.
An oak tree grew tall and strong
And raised her branches to God.

A robin built her downy nest
Among the leaves soft and deep.
Then nestled on the green breast,
She rocked her babies to sleep.

It's shaded a rippling brook
That fell from the mountainside;
And a wayfarer found his rest,
Just at the eventide.

Years passed, and lovers paused
Beneath that shade by the stream.
And the old oak tree stood silent
And listened to the lovers' dream.

If only I could leave for a while,
This world with its toils and care,
And hear once more a robin sing
From the old oak tree out there.

But my steps have grown so weary,
And soon my race will be run,
But through ages my tree will be
A haven from the burning sun.

Chris fished in the very shadow of the big oak tree, and now he lies in its shadow. At special times of the year, all of us––including his children—will put special things there. His children make things for him at school and place them on the stone upon which his marker sits. Things such as a heart attached to a Popsicle stick, painted with the words, "I love you." Special sayings for Father's Day, for Christmas—so many things we would like to talk about.

Our driveway passes by the cemetery, and so while driving down the driveway with Chris's children, even though it has been over four years since that day, we stop and roll down the windows, and the children say, "Hey, Daddy, I hit a home run today. We are going to Grammy's to spend the weekend." They often will talk with him about other things—such as something new that they may have received, or good grades in school—as though he hears them. I suppose he does sit in heaven and listen. We become quite emotional, and sometimes the children will ask, "Granddaddy, why is Grammy crying?" I simply say, "She misses your daddy." His youngest son does not remember his daddy but stands there beside the grave, looking down at the picture of him holding up two large fish with his cowboy hat on. So we tell him about his dad. His oldest son remembers his dad taking him fishing and all the good times of riding in the big truck.

Yes, we stand there to remember the days gone before. Memories are a wonderful thing. Markers are placed in cemeteries so we will not forget the person buried there. People design markers that exemplify the life of the one buried there. So it is with Chris, who loved to fish. His picture is on the marker with him holding up two big fish he had caught while wearing his favorite cowboy hat. Yes, there are memories of a life cut far too short.

CONCLUSION

There are so many things Betsy and I have learned in the rearing of our family. Every child is different, as we have already talked about. Different in so many ways—in looks, size, and in disposition. All have certain mannerisms about them. Mannerisms we as parents sometimes would like to change, but this is what makes the difference in each child. Children do not ask to be born into this world. Each one of us as parents made that decision for them. We cannot just tell God to take them back because they're just not working out.

Each one of us who has raised a family understands there will be struggles. Love each child as God has loved us. A child may not have mental illness or anything that would hinder his or her growing into adulthood, but all know there will be struggles along the way. When our children are born, there are going to be events in their lives we as parents did not bargain for. When these particular things come our way, we began to try to find the answer of how to overcome this problem.

Every child is different, and children are not to be discarded nor wished away, for they are a gift from God. Betsy and I never wished away Chris, just the problems. Wishing them away did not make them go away. We had to always try to find a solution, even when he became an adult. Is there any time in the raising of children that I as a parent can say, "My job is finished. I have raised my family, and they are all out of the nest now, and it's time to sit back and enjoy life"? Yes, there is an age children get to when they begin their own lives. We rejoice in that.

Late in the afternoon, after all the friends and family had departed, Betsy and I returned to the cemetery. We stood there looking at all the beautiful flowers, and Betsy took some to dry to put in a scrapbook. Today, all we can do is stand there and wish we could have done more. We stood next to the grave and looked at the fresh dirt that covered his casket. We remembered the words that were read from the Bible of how the body returns to that from which it came, and the spirit takes its flight back to God, who gave it. For Chris, he's at peace. There are no more burned lips from smoking crack; there is no more look of despair from not knowing what this day may bring forth. There are no more demons to be conquered. As Betsy said, "He's at peace." Yes, we were doing what so many have done before: standing next to someone we love and feeling useless. Death again had taken its toll upon someone who had so much to offer yet never could find what he was looking for. We are a normal family with ups and downs. Is your family like ours? I am sure it is. Every family must deal with certain struggles with their children. They may be different, but life is not always a rose garden. We all watch our children go through all the stages of life. You laugh, you cry, you rejoice. You discipline them when needed. We help with the homework and make them brush their teeth and eat their vegetables. As a family, we did all the normal things. We did everything right, or thought we did. What is right? What is enough? Enough is never enough.

Betsy and I raised five sons. We thought we could deal with any situation, any problem that might arise.

Yes, they all were different, and each had to find his place in the world. Some children will become teachers, others builders and truck drivers, and still others mechanics or farmers. Some, like Chris, never find what they are looking for, and so they turn to drugs, alcohol, and ultimately prison.

We, like so many who have gone down this same road, searched and played the blame game. Some marriages fail because one parent blames the other.

Stress is placed on marriages because someone has to pay for mistakes made. I cannot tell you that my wife and I did not have problems with this—we did. We never did discuss divorce, but we did have problems with how we should have handled Chris's situation. We talked about, and even argued about, what we should do with Chris, even at a very young age. Frustration runs high, and some marriages are put to the test, and many do not survive. The stress of living with someone with mental illness is hard. The stress of raising a family when conditions are normal is hard at times, but when other factors are added, then the stress meter starts climbing.

Let's all remember there can be no selfishness when it comes to taking care of our children. As parents, we are in this to the end. Our life is our children. One thing I have always preached and tried to practice is to never be selfish. Be a giver, not a getter. This will make us better parents, citizens of our communities, and above all, better Christians. Parents are to be givers, for children did not ask to be brought into this world. Good, bad, or indifferent, we as parents have a responsibility. Do not take it lightly. Sometimes the going is tough, and there just seems to be no light at the end of the tunnel, but we must deal with each task as it comes. Betsy and I gave it all we had, and in the end, well, it is all in God's hands now.

The boy was lost, bewildered, and alone;
He needed someone to lean upon.
He was too young to understand
Why you did not offer a helping hand.

The man was old, weak, and frail.
He needed warmth against the wintry gale.
You had no time for his aging feet,
Shuffling along on the busy street.

Somewhere close, you heard the cry
Of a lonely heart as you passed by.
You did not heed the sore distress
Of a voice crying in the wilderness.

You traveled on becoming discontent,
Then found out when your life was spent,
You had failed to leave from day to day
A part of yourself along the way.

You joined the band of the rushing throng,
Forgetting all others as you hurried along.
Then you ask of yourself the reason why
You had missed so much as life passed by.

—Thelma Brady